American Fathers

American Fathers

*A Tale of Intrigue,
Inspiration, and the
Entrepreneurial Spirit*

RON SCHUTZ
with Laura Baker

NEW YORK

NASHVILLE • MELBOURNE • VANCOUVER

American Fathers
A Tale of Intrigue, Inspiration, and the Entrepreneurial Spirit

Published in New York, New York, by Morgan James Publishing. Morgan James is a trademark of Morgan James, LLC. www.MorganJamesPublishing.com

The Morgan James Speakers Group can bring authors to your live event. For more information or to book an event visit The Morgan James Speakers Group at www.TheMorganJamesSpeakersGroup.com.

Disclosures: Ronald Schutz is a registered representative with a broker dealer and Registered Investment Advisor.

The opinions in this book are those of the author. Any financial recommendations in this book are part of the story and its characters and should not be taken as individual financial recommendations.

Profit Picture® is a trademark of Ron Schutz—Planning Business Transitions, LLC. 5225 Katy Freeway, Suite 430, Houston, TX 77007; 713-984-8044; www.ronschutz.com and www.profitpicture.net.

ISBN 978-1-68350-349-1 paperback
ISBN 978-1-68350-350-7 eBook
Library of Congress Control Number: 2016918828

Cover Design by:
Rachel Lopez
www.r2cdesign.com

Interior Design by:
Bonnie Bushman
The Whole Caboodle Graphic Design

In an effort to support local communities, raise awareness and funds, Morgan James Publishing donates a percentage of all book sales for the life of each book to Habitat for Humanity Peninsula and Greater Williamsburg.

Get involved today! Visit
www.MorganJamesBuilds.com

Dedication

To Pastor Eric Huffman, particularly for his Sept. 11, 2016, sermon on family (www.thestory.church), and to the voice of true patriots, people who embrace and strive to maintain the spirit of the Founding Fathers: Risk everything, expect no handouts, fail or succeed on your own results.

Contents

Preface

Finance is my profession, and politics is my sport. I spend time every day devouring the latest on each topic. When I found myself yelling at the TV and my computer during the first quarter of 2016, I realized it was time to speak up.

We're living in a time when regulations strangle initiative. Morality has no boundary. Common courtesy and respect for another individual is almost nonexistent. "What's in it for me?" is the mantra of many!

In my own business, I experience the impact of new regulations every day. The cost of doing business for myself and my clients begins to be prohibitive when we have to spend so much time and money meeting the demands of compliance, whether it's compliance to Department of Labor rules, such as how long your truck drivers can drive or how much you can pay your employees; the cost of health insurance even under ObamaCare (which promised to bring down the costs of medical care); Environmental Protection Agency regulations (which EPA is making outside the reach of Congress, the real law-making entity); and the list goes on. These are just a few examples of the factors contributing to the sluggish growth for our economy and stagnant wages for the majority of workers.

I watch the breakdown in Washington, D.C., where the discourse has become uncivil and no one entertains an idea unless it aligns with their own strident ideology. Our so-called representatives have forgotten that they represent a broad constituency and it's not about them getting re-elected. When I see our lawmakers holding a sit-in on the floor of Congress, all I can do is shake my head in disbelief. Where are the adults?

Going back and reading the original Federalist Papers and then reading the new biography of James Madison by Lynne Cheney, I can only imagine what our Founding Fathers must be thinking about the state of the United States.

Our Founding Fathers worked out their differences, often through compromise. They came back decades later to resolve issues still lingering. The USA has accomplished more economic advancement than any other civilization. What makes us great should be taught in schools, encouraged, and allowed to flourish. Compared with any other society, we have nothing to apologize for.

The individual businesspeople who create jobs locally are the ones who can help drive the change. If only they could make decisions that are good for their customers, their employees, and their families without so much government interference! The increased regulations that banks are subject to have limited the availability of capital for small to mid-sized businesses. I grew up in an era when the banker knew your character. He, or she, would make an informed decision based on your observed behavior. Today, regulators in Washington, D.C., set the rules based on academic criteria that they deem important without making adjustments for real-life application. The rule-makers suffer no consequences for the rules they perpetuate. The push for mandated increases in hourly wages is reducing customer service as owners are forced to find self-service or automated solutions to replace employees they can no longer afford.

All of us, if we trace back our ancestry, will soon find that our families came from someplace else. They generally entered the country to menial positions, congregated in tenements, assimilated, became more educated, and prospered. That is the American Dream. When I see people who are speaking in their native tongue to their children, I wonder if they are passing on their heritage and culture or if they are simply choosing to remain segregated from the rest of the English-speaking United States.

As I work with business owners, I find that they aren't always financially savvy and they are focused on other areas of their business. In today's "instant information" society, they want to know why they can't put their hands on financial information just as quickly as they can on most other kinds of information. We did something about that. We created Profit Picture™. It's an overlay on the firm's existing software systems to create visual representations of its financial data. My clients can now get what they want to know in 10 seconds. Making this available throughout the organization (filtering by management level or by role) creates a culture of transparency and accountability. When decisions are made at the field level within parameters set by owners, customers are better served and work gets done faster. For more information, visit www.profitpicture.net.

In our own organization, sometimes the best ideas come from the front lines—where the work is getting done. When every employee feels valued for their contribution, the team functions better as a unit.

In *American Fathers*, as you engage with Sasha and his efforts to find his way in American business, I hope you'll find some ideas to take back to your own workplace. It is also my hope that people will begin to create their own "idea networks" for solving problems at the lowest level in their company or in their communities with less oversight by regulatory agencies. Let's find a way to the solutions on our own without involving Washington.

—**Ron Schutz**, September 2016

Acknowledgments

I'd like to thank Laura Baker for helping me give each character a unique voice, Cindy Allen for her efforts to keep me on the straight and narrow, Jackie Lyles for introducing me to David Hancock at Morgan James Publishing, Mr. Hancock and his staff at for helping me create this final product, and George Abboud, my business partner, for collaborating, pushing me, and birthing Profit Picture™ (www.profitpicture.net). Our staff has been invaluable in providing time for this project: Adela Tischina, Aileen Castillo, Tracy Mulvey, and Jeannice Cain each in their own special way provided their talents to allow my professional life to run smoothly. Thank you all. I also thank my wife, Gail, for supporting me at work, at home, and throughout the creation of *American Fathers*. May the book teach all to respect one another now.

Chapter 1

Entrepreneurial Poet's
Solo Journey Begins

Knowledge will forever govern ignorance; and a people who mean to be their own governors must arm themselves with the power which knowledge gives.
—James Madison

S asha scratched his left leg in the back, just above the ankle. He was waiting for the Putney Station bus off of South Fulham Road in London. He could take the train, but as an American tourist, he preferred to watch the brightly clad schoolchildren crossing the road together, or observe the Chinese and African maids coming home from work. Sometimes—well, one time—he'd had a fairly nice conversation with one of the Chinese maids. She was a younger woman around 30 and wearing a red plaid skirt. She was still six years or so older than he was but, he had hoped, young enough to banter with him in Mandarin. He was right, and they'd chatted and laughed lightly all the way to Brixton, where she got off to cook and clean for her own family.

A year and a half ago, a holiday in London at 23 had sounded just right to him as he accepted the Longhorn Poetry Fellowship from the University of Texas at Austin along with his BS diploma in business. "The Entrepreneurial Poet" was a name he sometimes called himself. He enjoyed thinking of himself in the third person. His mother had had a habit of doing this during his childhood. She would say as if reading from a book, "Her son had bright brown eyes but this did not prevent him from falling down a lot." As he went out the door to the graduation ceremony, she had said, "He stands ready to be created."

"*Ana* was the Uyghur word for *mother*," he thought to himself. He called her name in his heart. "Ana . . . where are you? Have you left me alone?" Sasha was 25 now, and the events of the intervening 18 months had made the postponed London trip more desirable than ever . . . even necessary.

The double-decker bus pulled up and Sasha pulled down tightly on his gray wool toboggan hat. No need to attract attention. He was average height and could pass for a college student from the States. He was from the States. He was an American. It had been 13 years since he stood with his parents in the crowded Austin courtroom and solemnly pledged his allegiance to the United States of America. His mother, Nur Ye, had held his left hand. His father, Yusup Sabir, had kept him near. He was like most Uyghur sons, a protected child. Before ethnic cleansing by the Han Chinese, the Uyghur people had lived in the rocky regions of China bordering Kyrgyzstan. Once he started school in Austin, Sasha had quickly learned to simply refer to himself as "Chinese." Loved, pampered, pushed to academic excellence at all times, he had never questioned his parents' love. Not really. His mother had sometimes whispered in his ear as she looked at his father, "You are his castle he is building to live in."

When you face certain and horrible death and you miraculously escape to a wide, green field full of flowers, you do not question anything. Your family is still alive, and a future lies ahead of you. That is enough. Later, he realized, he was their future. That is what his mother meant when she whispered in his ear.

The bus meandered along Fulham Road up toward the Kensington District. He watched the line of jewelry stores, chemists, and, every five blocks, a KFC or Starbucks: ah, home.

His father had been glad to see him leave for London, glad to release him to the world. This man, who had pulled him, a little boy, with him out of the Xinjiang region where his part-Chinese, part-Turkish, part-Arabic tribe was being massacred by the Han Chinese, this man he called "Chichi," meaning "Daddy," he realized now, had been anxiously awaiting the day when they could say goodbye.

The events that led to his father pushing him out of the nest were so upsetting to Sasha that he never talked about them. No one else knew except for the three of them—his mother, his father, and him—the reasons why they were no longer a family.

The day after graduation, he had gone skiing—water skiing—a new sport he'd discovered when a girl asked him out. He didn't tell them that a girl, Julia, had asked him out. He just said, ". . . some friends from my accounting class." That day, he met Julia on campus, and she drove them to Lake Travis, about a half-hour away, where they joined six others. Julia spotted her friend's boat, and they jumped aboard. When Sasha's turn came, he slipped on the skis in the tepid green water, adjusted his vest, grabbed the rope handles, and waved his hand for them to take off, and they went flying. Flying was a joy, like poetry.

When he woke in the hospital, he had a crease in his skull from where the boat and it had collided. Not his friend's boat, another boat nearby that caught him in a wide arc.

"Your hair will cover the scar," his mother said as her fingers caressed his face. Her fingers were so small, yet he'd seen them throw a knife 20 feet and kill a duck in midair. Her fingers traveled over his head as if she could magically bring back the thick black hair that had once covered it.

❧

The bus suddenly jolted to a stop and snapped Sasha out of his painful memories.

He scanned the busy streets for his maid "friend." The domestic workers did not usually board until 3:30, and it was just now 3:00, the hour of sunset in wintry England. In one hour, the streetlamps would be on. The question that was never far from his mind, reasserting itself over and over, was, "Where is my mother now?"

Sasha leaned back against the bus seat and let his mind wander back again to the days after his accident.

Nur Ye and Yusup had taken him home. Soup—they gave him soup and dumplings. His father rubbed his toes. They stroked his bald, bandaged head and told him stories from the mountains about caves and kings. A week passed. His mother put the gray cap on his head "to keep the bandages safe," she said. She alone changed them. He wore the hat. He slept in the hat. After eight weeks, he took the hat off to dress his own wounds. He was a grown man, after all. He could do it himself.

Then something fantastical happened. On his once off-white skull grew a forest of tiny reddish orange swirls. Was it a disease? He gasped at his reflection. A parasite? A reaction to the medicine? He reached up and touched it, just as he did now unconsciously in his bus seat. One ruddy ringlet bounced happily out from under his cap before he pushed it back.

It wasn't long before Yusup spied the red curls. "Red-haired Uyghur boy! Chinese redhead!" His father, who saw that he was *just another boy* and not a son from his loins after all, raged through their apartment shouting in the language he knew the neighbors did not know. Sasha bowed his head like a child. He felt guilty for ruining the castle his father had spent so many years building. Tears streamed down his face, "Chichi . . . Chichi . . . ." But Yusup would not, could not contain his fury and loss.

"Chichi, Chichi," he cried again and again outside of his parents' bedroom door, but they were fighting and did not hear him. Then, he was afraid for his mother. He heard crashing sounds and cries. His father would beat her. This was the common way in China. He pushed open the door, but she stood unharmed, tying a scarf over her head.

His father, at the far end of the room yelled at him, "Go!"

"No." His mother's voice sounded slightly different. He realized that she was speaking in English and no longer had an accent. "I am going." She walked out with nothing. She never came back.

They stood in the apartment together, he and Yusup, for a few minutes after she left, and then Sasha ran out the door to find her and bring her back. He ran down one street and then another, his chest heaving for air in the muggy spring night. She had not taken the car; surely, she was walking. He ran. He ran for one hour and then two. Eventually, he just ran aimlessly. He ran all night, calling out her name, up and down little streets with the names of hardwood trees: Maple, Birch, Aspen, Oak, Pecan. How could someone disappear into thin air? He ran past grocery stores and insurance agencies. He ran past car washes and Vietnamese restaurants, the word "Mother" falling out of his mouth between breaths.

Finally, at dawn, Sasha stopped at a Shell station and bought some water. He leaned against the wall behind the station and then crumpled to the ground as his head suddenly seemed to split open with a throbbing pain. He waited, halfway reclined, to see if blood came out of his nose. It didn't. He checked his stitches. Still holding. He waited for an hour, hoping that he would be able to walk home, his legs sprawled out onto the asphalt helplessly.

That is how the police found him. They asked him his name and radioed in that they had found the missing man. He vaguely registered that Yusup had reported him missing and injured. The officers helped Sasha up to the front door, and Yusup took him in and laid him on his narrow boy's bed. For five days, he slept and woke, only to sleep again. In his dreams, he was chasing a white owl far ahead in the sky. Then he would be in a barn with the owl, but the barn had so many windows and doors, there was no way to keep an owl inside. Sometimes, mountain lions and bears roared outside the barn, just like the wild animals he had heard as a child in China, and Sasha would be afraid and wake up.

Yusup came and went with soup and tea and cookies. He had the face of a suddenly wifeless, childless man: sunken and pressed into something unspeakable. He could not stop loving Sasha, he could not forgive Nur. How could she steal his castle from him—he, a simple man who had never beat her like the other husbands beat their wives? He had brought her to the United States, her and her son. Sasha could almost hear Yusup beating his chest in the wail of grief as he moved quietly about the apartment.

After five days, Sasha sat up and then stood up. He stretched his arms above his head. Here he was, and he would have to face what fate had brought him. He felt the power of youth ripple through his forearms and his mind went immediately to Yusup. "I must take care of him. He is still my father," he thought, and he cleaned the kitchen and made dinner in a kind of funeral ritual. The ceremony of their family life was past. This was a new ceremony, one of mourning and one of new beginnings. Sasha made dumplings and spicy eggs, Yusup's favorite dishes. He had the meal ready when he heard the key in the lock and the thin figure came in.

Yusup only paused for a moment and then bowed slightly and went to wash his hands.

In the weeks and months that followed, his father was not unkind to him. They ate together at table every night. They talked sometimes of his father's work in a municipal lab testing water. He was not able to practice as a dentist, his profession in China, in the United States. Sometimes, over dinner, Sasha read him a headline. Theirs was the talk of the voiceless.

Yusup's eyes were small and black. He could see many things about a person, he often said, from their teeth. Sasha and Nur used to laugh when he described, in a mock-serious tone, the man who chewed grass blades and straw like a cow or the woman who ground her teeth to nubs because her sister had a bigger house. In the year since his mother left them, Yusup's face had grown sallow and his eyes, blank. Sasha cooked for him and took him walking by the lake. When Sasha told him that he was going to London, his father looked down and cried, "You are still my son." He bowed to his father and held his shrinking frame in his long arms. He wondered if Yusup would die of a broken heart .

On the way to the airport, Yusup began to speak to him in a quiet voice, "When you come back, you will have a brother. I marry Yu Hong Yi tomorrow. She is . . . . It is a boy."

So, his father would not die. He wasn't as weak and sad as he had seemed. Sasha was not *really* still his son. Nothing was as it seemed. He swallowed several times, then decided, as children often do, to say out loud what is embarrassing. "I'm not going to let you throw me away, Chichi. I don't care what you do, you can't just throw me away."

Yusup steered the car over to the side of the road and stopped. His hands began to shake, and he took them off of the steering wheel and put them on top of Sasha's head. He smiled, and Sasha could see the perfect rows of shiny teeth he had carefully cultivated to gain new dental business in China. "Sasha, I love you. You . . . you are in my heart, but I need to have a baby. Please understand."

Sasha nodded, obedient and pacified. "OK," he said.

"I'm not throwing you away. I have two sons now." Yusup held up two fingers as if he were talking to a little boy.

"OK, Chichi." Sasha shrugged. He was defeated. There was no way he could keep his family from disintegrating like soap suds in his hands. "OK." They drove on to the airport, and he got out of the car screaming inside. He grabbed his bags, waved, and walked away. It was the kind of walk away that it takes a lifetime to make; Sasha moved with a tall, lanky grace away from the man in the car and into the airport terminal.

Now, here he was, riding the bus through London while inside he was still walking away, waving goodbye.

The London bus stopped and Sasha jumped up, pushing all thoughts of his recent past out of his mind. He got off the bus near St. James Park . He tried to clear his head and simply enjoy the evening. He was now in the heart of London, walking in near darkness. A horse stood on the other side of a fence in a little stable; he couldn't see it, but he could hear it snorting and moving against the walls of its stall as he passed. Vast hills stretched away as he entered the great gardens of the city. An old man walked by, a mother met her young daughter on the path and they turned toward home in the twilight, talking of school. He pulled out his pad and wrote:

Bastard is an English word
woven from bard and bested.
Long gowns, kingly staffs of state,
still the crowning heads are boys,
begotten by strange men.
Unnamed chancellor,
stallion on the foggy Eve.
'Tis the lark,
No, 'tis the nightingale
Lovers' game, lovers' gnome.
Little boy, go home.

There was no one, which suited Sasha, and he walked, gray hat pulled low, across all the bridges of London that night. London whispers in the wee hours after the pubs close. Barely a tree cracks or an owl screeches. Too soon, before daylight, the people flow out of their houses again, onto the buses and trains.

At dawn, Sasha was back at St. James Park and caught the same bus back up Fulham Road toward his rented room in the attic of an old London boarding house. An ageless bus driver sat at the helm. White curls and a belly hinted at a nature softer than the one he projected. He was round and spoke quite sternly to boarding passengers about tokens and moving back from the front of the bus and talking on their cell phones. Sasha sat on the front seat near the driver. There was a fresh newspaper on the seat, and he opened it. A white paper fluttered out from its folds onto the rubber floor mat. Lifting the paper, he put it back in its hiding place without opening it. He was, after all, a careful, red-haired Chinese boy.

The driver had rosy cheeks and might have been called jolly if he had not had such a no-nonsense way about him. He warned the drunken sailor and his swaying friend—sporting a keffiyeh, the traditional Saudi headdress—to keep it down. They saluted and put their tokens in. This was high drama, Sasha had learned, for the English. Certainly, it was far more interesting than the automatic trains and flirtatious woman's voice announcing stations in the London Underground: Knightsbridge, Green Park, Piccadilly Circus.

He thought as he traveled down Fulham Road to his stop at Putney Bridge that the white folded paper he'd found would be an invoice, perhaps, or a legal deposition, an inventory or a banker's résumé. It was none of these things.

When he opened it, leaning against the dormer window in his room, he read, "*Sasha.*" Disturbed, he put the letter down. It was a letter, after all. He closed the curtains and locked his door. Someone was following him. What else could it be? Breathlessly crouching on the bed and gazing to see if there was a shadow in the hallway, he continued reading.

Everything I am going to tell you in this letter is the truth. I do not usually tell the truth about my past. In fact, the only other time in my memory I have done so was when I knew Nur in 1991. "Nur" is your mother's name . . . I think. It is the name she told me. We met in Athens. We were both working for our governments—she for China, and I was an operative for the USSR. You might say, in your American way, that we had the same beat but different bosses. Our love story is too precious for me to put down here and now. Yes, I loved her. She said she loved me. We were even married, although that was so dangerous and tricky, and we had to part so soon afterwards that sometimes I can't believe it happened. They took her away to another location. I didn't know she was married to your father or that you had been born for some time—not until you were seven or eight.

She recently sent me a message. She said you are my son. Normally, I am not quite so blunt, but I said I would be honest about my past.

My name is Victor. You can write to me care of the No. 93 Route, but only when the driver with the curly white hair is behind the wheel, first bus seat. Please burn this letter.

V.

The red-haired Chinese son of spies did not burn the letter. Instead, he threw it on the floor. In his clothes and without a bite to eat, he lay down. As the clock struck nine, sleep took him.

Chapter 2

Red-Headed Stepchild Makes a Plan

Religious bondage shackles and debilitates the mind and unfits it for every noble enterprise, every expanded prospect.
—James Madison

In the three days that followed Sasha's discovery of Victor's letter, he wrote 48 poems. It was a manifesto of poetry, each building on the last until he completed what he now knew was his first book, with a haiku:

No. 48
Iron bridge iced
Footsteps sliding, hands bite rails
Rust wears me, I him.

When he finished writing, he took the 15:00 Putney Bridge bus. He had a letter for this man who claimed to be his father. Actually, Sasha believed Victor. He realized that he had known for a long time that his mother had a secret life. She had often let down her guard in front of him when he was a little boy, and he remembered clearly hearing her speak Turkish, Russian, and even Dutch on the phone—always when Yusup was gone. He only identified the languages later when he heard them again. He saw her laughing at Arabic jokes on the square. How could a Chinese housewife, so young, speak so many languages? She had taught him when he was eight the poetry of Rumi, the Hindi songs , and the German lines of Rilke. Of course, he never questioned that his mother or his father, who taught him chemistry and how to climb a mountain, knew all things.

As Sasha sat on his bed in the London attic considering his life thus far, he saw that he had been given much. He could not complain. Victor's appearance added another layer of richness to his life, he was certain. "The more man meditates upon good thoughts, the better will be his world and the world at large." Common Confucian wisdom echoed in his ears.

Now, he must get down to business: money, work, plans, and purpose. The stuff of economies and inventions interested him, and he had a suspicion that Victor was just the person to give his ideas a bruising review. Victor hadn't insulted him, but Sasha could feel the pricking of a sharp intelligence just below the surface of his words. His mother always said, "Only trust the person who insults you; they are probably telling the truth."

Dear Victor, Sir:

    I bow to you, my second father. I am honored that you reach out to me, a stranger, in reality.

    Certainly, Sir, I have many questions. You may not be aware of my current situation. It is because of my current situation that I would like to wait to ask you my many questions about the past and my mother. Instead, I take the risk of offending you by being presumptive and submitting to you a sketch of my life plan in the hopes that you will offer me your thoughts.

    My situation is this: My mother has left Yusup and me. Neither of us have any knowledge of her whereabouts for the last year or so. Yusup has fathered a son and taken a new wife. Perhaps I would be welcome in their home, but I do not think so. I am a 25-year-old graduate with $5,000 and a plane ticket back to Texas in 25 days. My work experience has been exclusively testing water in the Austin city lab where Yusup works and teaching a few classes on Third World economies. I speak and write five languages. I have just finished *my first book of poetry. With no home and no job, I must land on my feet. Here are some of my thoughts.*

You are most gracious to consider my request. I value your gift of honest insight. Please do not spare my feelings, as I cannot afford such comforts at the moment. I have some sense of business from my studies, but I am naïve enough to think that I have not taken various costs and obstacles into account.

Sincerely yours,
Sasha

PLAN [First Incarnation]

Vision: To change the world using both poetry and a "water reader" invention.

Mission: To continue to write poetry that investigates the fiber of American morality. To create an invention that instantly "reads" water right out of the well or the tap and will also instantly test seawater: not only for just the usual bacteria count and nitrate, mineral levels, but also for pharmaceutical cocktails, probable household cleaners, and industrial discharge. This invention will shock citizens and their governments into changing their behavior around the purchase and disposal of water, thus creating a safer environment for humans and all biology.

Because of the instant results, seawater-to-freshwater conversion will be safer.

Stage 1 [6 months]:
- Get a job ASAP in a water-testing or water-treatment plant near the Pacific or Atlantic oceans.
- Publish my first book: *Weaver Number One.*
- Triple my $5,000 in savings by:
  a. saving half of income,
  b. investing and trading,
  c. saving 50% of earnings of pre-release book sales,
  d. recording audio file of book to sell online.

Stage 2 [1 year]:
- Set up a home laboratory and begin scientific tests toward the invention of the water reader.
- Continue work on second book.
- Publish second book.
- Triple my $15,000 savings by above stated methods as well as sale of highly oxygenated [active] water to research facilities. [Byproduct of testing.]

Stage 3 [1 year]:
- Publish scientific findings and patent invention. [Cost of global patents = $60,000—borrow against savings to establish credit.]
- Solicit investors to manufacture prototype.
- Test prototype in three American cities.
- Incorporate and quit job.
- Pay off debt at the end of the year.
- Begin consulting work and use travel to promote books. [Sign with agency or ?]
- Triple savings of $45,000 by activities noted above as well as expanded water sales, book sales, and speaking jobs.

Stage 4 [2 years]:
- Complete prototype tests and begin selling water reader to municipalities, hospitals, and finally to the general public via grocery store distribution and YouTube. [Goal is for overhead to equal no more than 25% of sales.]
- Strategic marketing campaign in Australia to save the Great Barrier Reef from extinction by ridding the sea of chemical cleaners that are bleaching it.
- Set total 1st-year sales goal of $2 million; net $1 million.
- Work out production facility, material, and labor costs. Other costs?
- Save $2 million from increased investment dividends, small real estate, currency-exchange trading, and 50% of consulting and speaking fees.

> • Start nonprofit micro-lending after Grameen Bank model in high child poverty index areas of the United States: rural Texas, Arkansas, Mississippi, and Louisiana.
> • Get married?

He slipped his reply into the folded newspaper on the front seat of the bus and got off at Kensington Gardens, where his feet often haunted the paths at night. The world was a wonder to him on this momentous day of his first book—and his first letter to Victor. He passed the stables at dusk and listened to the rustling leaves. Knowing that these three adults, his mother, his father, and Victor, circled around his past and present made him happy.

With his letter "mailed," his book finished, and his mind free to wander with his feet, Sasha found himself near the palace at midnight. Was the Queen asleep in there, he wondered, or did she slip into the parks at night as he did, draped in an old wool coat and a housedress, like a night cleaner or a woman from the country come to town to drop off her fresh veggies at the posh houses? He nodded to the guards and decided to slip over to Crandall's.

Paddy Crandall lived in the private apartment of an exclusive club. His apartment had an outside entrance with a small balcony facing the palace. Sasha had met Crandall several months ago there. Only an American, Crandall said, would knock on someone's door at three o'clock in the morning just to ask for a cup o' tea. Sasha remembered their meeting. He would never forget it.

That night, as he passed Crandall's window, Sasha caught a full view of the man sitting in his chair enjoying Beethoven. He was an arm's length away from the dark street, but lost in another world of sweeping music. Sasha stood and stared at the amiable-looking fellow, wrapped in dark blue, with a long, white beard and sunken into a giant red velvet chair. Almost, he realized later, almost like Santa Claus. Sasha had spent an hour or so knocking about late-closing pubs and little stores. He felt so alone in the world and especially alone in London, which went to bed quite early in January. He had knocked on Crandall's door, just as he said, at three o'clock in the morning. He'd been afraid to knock, and at the same time, he didn't care about propriety. He was willing to risk the wrath of a man who might just be a kindred spirit.

Crandall, his white beard flying around his wool Japanese house coat, flung open the door wildly. There on his stoop was a thin Asian lad with timid, peering eyes, a gray wool cap pressed down to his face. Normally, he wouldn't have done this, but something about the poor fellow propelled Crandall to invite him in for some tea and whisky. When he found out that this waif was a poet, they'd had a lively discussion about who was better, John Donne or all of the French poets.

Crandall had a lively mind and a great deal of knowledge about financial matters, philosophy, and spiritual topics. He sat back at one point and asked to hear some of Sasha's poems. After the first one, he asked to hear another and then another. He was the consummate listener and host, showing great kindness. As Sasha recited his poems to this new-found friend, he felt the millions of twinges of fear of offending, fear of errors, and fear of bragging—all pressed into him by his careful parents. He felt them fall away in the warmth of Crandall's acceptance and interest.

Crandall was a businessman alone in London. He was doing some banking business and waiting in his London club apartment to join his wife once she set up house somewhere in the country. Crandall had stuffed Sasha full of potatoes, beans, and eggs before pushing him toward the door, laughingly urging, "Go on now, get your rest." Sasha hated to leave such a haven. He smiled his biggest smile, half bowed, half shook Crandall's hand, and trod off into the morning.

Sasha's mind was dwelling on that wonderful early-morning meeting this midnight when he saw Crandall's light burning bright. Just as before, Sasha could see him fully from the street, this time huddled over his table reading a newspaper. Sasha knocked, and after the great rush of welcome from what felt like an old friend, he was ushered into the room and into Crandall's thoughts.

"Did you know that they got a tax on those of you Americans who come here to the UK to get medical operations?" Crandall asked. Sasha shook his head. "The UK makes money on that already. Why make you poor buggers pay out the nose to get your nose job?" Crandall had a smile that fought with his cheeks to be seen. He smiled now, which transformed and lightened the room. "HA! HA!"

Sasha laughed involuntarily, caught up in the man's good humor, and sat down in a chair by the table.

Crandall quickly placed a hot cup of tea in front of him. "Look what the club cook gave me! Nearly half a molasses cake." Crandall was putting out the plates and arranging what looked like warm brandy sauce in a little pitcher. Sasha had already learned that when it came to entertaining, Crandall enjoyed making a fuss over his guest. His eyes twinkled as he brought out a broad slice of black sticky cake and set it down before Sasha. He then poured a good bit of sauce all over the cake, soaking it and adding a flourish of raisins. He stroked his great, white beard and said, "Now, let us break cake together."

Sasha was not one to suffer with moods or loneliness, but there had been tests to his even-mindedness lately. He did miss the warmth of friends and family while on his sojourn in wintry London. He found that he was continuously reeling internally over the explosion of his family; he still could not grasp the change from being the adored son of two parents to being a homeless orphan. He was unsettled, as they say, in all of his movements, and he couldn't find a way to reconcile his losses. That is how he saw the changes that had occurred—as losses.

Sasha ate the cake and stretched out his feet.

Crandall was nestled back in his red chair. He leaned forward, his eyes alight with curiosity. "So, tell me," he said. "What is going on in your life, Sasha? Are you writing poems? Have you spoken with Yusup? Where have you been in the city since we last met?"

There is nothing like presenting yourself when you are a young person to a seasoned adult whom you admire and trust. Then, you often catch the first sounds of your own convictions.

Sasha pulled out his new book and handed it to Crandall.

"What's this?" Crandall opened it slowly.

"It's my first book. I just finished it."

"Ah." Crandall nodded, his bushy eyebrows dancing with happiness. Sasha laughed. It burst out of him before he knew it. His intuition told him that

Crandall would be delighted with him, no matter what he created, whether it be a book or a soufflé. He was unconditionally interested in whatever Sasha cared about.

Crandall began to read the book in his hands, quietly humming and reading, humming and reading. Sasha leaned back in his chair against the wall and closed his eyes. For this moment in time, he was going to call this place "home."

When Sasha finally left Crandall's apartment and boarded the bus again, it was six o'clock in the morning. There was a newspaper on the front seat, but it was empty. The bus, crammed with students and Ukrainian shop girls, seemed to rock a bit. Sasha thought about his plan. Would he make it? He remembered Yusup showing him the way to climb a mountain in the dangerous Kazakhstan region. "Stay flat, stay still," he said. "Move one foot slowly, up, always up: around and up, side and up, down and up, inside and up. You go up."

"What if I'm afraid of falling?" he asked him, eyes on the faraway ground.

"You go up," Yusup said, leaving no doubt about what he expected from his son. "When you get to the top, then you go down a different way."

"Why do I go a different way?" He was already estimating the risk.

His father shrugged and grinned and said, "For fun."

Sasha opened the door to his room on Fulham Road and threw himself on the bed. On his mind right then was the exchange rate of the Chinese Yuan. He wondered if he dared bet on it with some of his money. He knew that he could trade currency without a license, if he went under a bank umbrella. He started to dial a German friend who might help him, but sleep tugged his head down to the pillow, and there he sank. His last thought before drifting off to sleep was, "How much does my skull weigh with my brain in it?"

Sasha slept through the morning and woke at noon. It was cloudy and rainy. It was quiet. He thought of trying to make a bowl of ramen in the kitchen before the landlady appeared. She frowned on boarders using the kitchen, which seemed odd to him.

Without moving from the bed, he lay musing, relishing the time to relax before he sprang into action.

Most things in England, he found, were quite a bit more restricted than in the United States. Wifi wasn't free, veggies were wrapped in small packages for you at the grocery store, a taxi cost $100 every 10 miles, forcing people to use more public transportation. People were friendly-ish but not quite warm. Many of the people his age whom he overheard talking in cafes were unemployed—job opportunities were less, they had to get by on less. They were looking for work and getting leads from a government agency. Still, it was surprising to learn that they could be unemployed and have no concerns about becoming homeless, lacking medical care, or even going hungry. It was shocking, in a way, to discover that the horror of losing one's job was gone. Just gone. He wondered what these Brits had to give up to get such peace of mind.

His parents had not discussed politics with him directly. They did talk about being openly disgusted by the waste they found in the United States, though. Furniture, carpets, clothes, and many other things were simply discarded, it seemed to Nur and Yusup, when they still had a long and useful life ahead. "In China, we use same furniture our whole life," Yusup had said, pointing to a giant furniture store one day in disbelief. "How much they have to sell every day to stay in business?"

"Remember, Yusup, how we had to stand so often in the houses," Nur reminded him. "Our chairs in China were broken. Still, I see food in the trash." This was their economy—the economy of the home and the family. Communism was not as good as capitalism, they knew. At the same time, they missed it somehow. They missed, he thought, being told what to think.

He chuckled and thought, "A real big brother who bosses you around, and you can grow fond of."

He heaved his body off the bed, shook out the blankets, and straightened his pillow. That's when he saw the corner of the letter. He knew what it was. When did Victor come in here? Was he sleeping? A chill ran through his body. Had he entered his room before he even got home? Damn spies.

Sitting down, he opened it. It was thick—four typed pages, at least. Part of him sighed in relief even as the other part stepped back. Was this OK? For Victor to enter his room uninvited? He wondered if Victor had gone through his things. Did he see that he had not burned the first letter? He began to read.

My Dear Sasha,

Certainly, I would expect you to be formulating a plan. Time is of the essence, not only in terms of your current cash flow but also because you are a young man who must make his way. When I was your age, I wanted to be a senator. I was enraptured with the classical times, the stories of Socrates and Plato making speeches and affecting the hearts and minds of Greece. I woke up to a harsh reality as I entered college, however. The Russian government was simply a kind of mafia, a one-party administration. The only speeches were those written for the speakers by censors. Power lay with cunning and might. I could have found a trade, I suppose, like my father, and made metal frames for buildings or surveyed land. For some reason, I think because I was often bullied at school, I wanted to be a spy, a man who tricked people and who could commit crimes with impunity. Little did I know of the darkness that awaited me or the crimes I would commit against myself.

You write to me of free enterprise. Did you stop to think that I might not have any experience in free enterprise? After all, I was a member of the Communist Party. But, you are right. Many people in Russia are great capitalists. We invent, market, buy and sell, all in clandestine ways. Money flows freely in and around the laws that are supposed to prevent it from flowing.

I started my career as an undercover agent by following and reporting on the movements of a high-ranking East German official. This was in the late seventies. The man was not an easy target. He had many secret meetings and often made coded phone calls. Nevertheless, I believe that I tracked his every movement very well. That is what I thought. One night, I awoke to see him sitting at the foot of my bed. I was your age, 25. "Victor," he spoke to me in a familiar way, as one would to a son. He was in his late fifties. "I see you are a 'green man,' new to this world of espionage. Perhaps they gave you this job because it was not so important. By that I mean that we are, that East Germany, is falling, is failing. We will not be here much longer."

By this time, I had found my gun and was readying my finger on the trigger, when he smiled and said very gently, "Put your gun down, please.

I'm not going to hurt you. I'm here to make a deal. Would you like to know what sort of deal before you kill me?"

I sat up slowly and laid my gun on top of the blanket. He took no notice of it. *"Listen. Do not speak. I know all about you and I . . . we believe that you are the person we have been looking for. There is a sort of 'commission' for you, if you will do this for us."*

"You speak in riddles," I finally whispered to him, hoarse with embarrassment.

"Don't be embarrassed," he said. (I will call him Herr Bourecher.) *"We, that is, the government of East Germany, we have some assets that we would like to see stored in a safe place for the time being. You see, things have become unstable. We are looking for a friend, a sort of invisible friend, who will carry our . . . assets quietly away, watch them in a safe place and bring them back when the time is right."*

I turned my head to look around me. I could not risk speaking out loud. How did he take such a risk? I did not know at the time how many people were around me, how many agents had combed my room, tested my clothing and shoes, and even taken apart my floor, walls and ceiling. Indeed, I did not know many things.

The short of it, Sasha, is that I became a sort of double agent right away . . . on my first job. I agreed to transport gold bullion out of East Germany and into Switzerland without alerting my Russian superiors. Herr Bourecher made it easy for me by traveling there himself, and so I followed him with my hidden load. Once in neutral territory, I went into hiding. It's hard to hide from the Russians, but, of course, one can if one is creative. It helps to live underground, and it is even better to live inside an obscure mountain in a place with no roads.

In 1989, I returned the bullion to the East Germans minus a few agreed-upon million Deutsche Marks, which were deposited in a Swiss account. I tell you all of this, Sasha, so that you can understand how I, a one-time Communist, learned about financial investing without working a massive crime or black market operation. That is simply not my style. I was in hiding for nearly five years, reading Plato and herding *goats. I lived in a cave with a candle and an oil heater. In this strange way, I accumulated capital. When I returned to Russia in 1994, things were much more lax, as you can imagine, after the fall of Communism. They still needed researchers and semi-secret operatives, however, and I thought working for the Russians would serve as a great cover for my entrepreneurial schemes.*

I bought into a legitimate shipping firm and began to deal in overseas distribution of goods.

Here are my first thoughts about your plan:

1. Excellent ideas. Dream big. You need to stick with it until it stops working and then drop it fast. If it keeps working, stay with it. Make as many changes as you need to make. Don't let your ego tell your wallet what to do.

2. Here is a list of obstacles I believe you will encounter:

   - Taxes—In the United States, they tax every single penny you save and earn. They also tax you in other ways: fees for use, permission, ownership and legal filings. You say that you will sell a byproduct of your experiments to make money. Will you be declaring this profit on your taxes? Will you be complying with clean preparation standards by the Medical or Industrial Product Safety Regulations? Check into this, and find out what sort of penalties you will have to pay if you are caught violating the regulations.

   - Patents—Factor the price of patents into your budget. Every country requires a patent, and the filing fees cost thousands, as does the patent attorney.

   - Medical insurance—You say that you will have a job. Will your employers pay for your medical insurance? How much? How much will you be required to pay, even if you don't want to buy medical insurance?

   - Retirement—Will your employers force you to invest part of your money in a 401K or some other sort of retirement plan like Social Security? Of course they will. How will you adjust for that loss, and how can you keep as much as possible? Is there a way to get the money out of the system after you leave your job?

- Business structure—Think about what sort of business structure you want before you solicit investors. How much control do you want? FYI, they will want all the control if they pay you to create the prototype.
- Investing and saving—Here are my thoughts on this: LUCK, something I learned in a Don Blanton workshop.

L stands for *liquidity*. Having cash can give you strong negotiating power. Next time you are looking at a purchase after coming to a potential agreed-upon price, say simply, "If I wrote you a check now how much would you knock off?" If it is not in the 5% or greater discount range, walk away.

U stands for *use*. You should be able to access the money simply and easily without a hassle. An example of what would not work well is when you make an investment that is meant for a longer term or that may have a penalty if you withdraw money before a certain age or time frame. You want something that is easily convertible to cash.

C is for *control*. If the government sets the rules in plans like 401K that postpone taxes without telling you what you owe and only allows you complete control without penalty from age 59½ to age 70½, that is a very small window that may not fit with your personal plans. Yet radio and TV are loaded with recommendations to "maximize" your deferred (postponed tax bill) savings. You lose control. So, find an investment plan that gives you some control all the time and doesn't penalize you for accessing your money when you want it.

Finally, K is for *knowledge*. There is so much misinformation or incomplete information on the Internet. Be sensible. I suggest that you have at least three months of emergency-fund money in a highly liquid account. You will generally pay taxes on the returns from that account each year.

Allocate funds for "safe money," which has little or no risk of downside loss. I have personally found that high early cash value life insurance with living riders can be an attractive option as part of a financial back-up plan.

Allocating funds for risk money is next, depending on your risk budget (tolerance for loss). If you do not have consumer debt (credit card, lease payments or other non-deductible debt) and your employer matches your contribution, and if you can wait until age 59½ to access these funds, consider a 401K. Use this allocation for risk because taxes are postponed, and making changes within the first year will not potentially double—or more—the part that goes to the IRS. Put those last two words together, and what do you get? "TheIRS."

A professional advisor who is properly licensed to provide advice on financial products is well worth the average 1% or so they charge. Making a mistake can cost you many multiples higher in taxes. Taxes are, in fact, your largest transaction cost. The professional need not be a CFP. A CPA is not an investment professional. They do taxes. An attorney handles legal-contract issues, not financial ones. A banker wants you to borrow money at a "rental" rate called interest. They are not financial professionals, so don't ask for or follow their financial advice.

Being paid for time is predictable; there's relatively little accountability for effort. Your only limit is the time you put in. Results-based rewards normally generate greater wealth. Creating a pharmaceutical-content water tester that is easy to use and reliable can create wealth to do good without government controlling your every move. Believe me, I know how that feels, to have the government control my every move.

Sasha, there's so much more I would like to add, so very much more, especially about Nur, but this letter is becoming a book, isn't it? I will stick to the practical for now, as you requested. You were a sheltered child, and now you must make your own way. Let me share some of my observations about growing wealth in American society when you start with nothing.

First of all, be careful that you work as a nonexempt employee and refuse offers to become a manager. Americans are like children who have figured out that hard work and innovation make money. They keep pulling that lever and money comes out. Older societies know that there is much more to success than simply producing wealth, goods and services. You must have rest and spare time. You must not feel that you are always in a race, and you must have a way into and out of a job if you need it, without suffering huge losses.

The greatest thing you can imagine is not a new invention that will make money, even though that is wonderful. The greatest thing that you can imagine is how your fellow human must feel. Capitalism in the United States is under siege right now, and the only thing that can save it is following this piece of advice: "Love your neighbor as yourself." You may find that hard to believe, but I will talk more about it with you soon.

Getting back to working for an hourly wage. When you do this, you can at least have a sense of fairness and balance in your life. Exempt employees are told to travel, work nights and weekends and generally suck up the loss margins of the company into their own lives. So, you run your life. Make friends, but keep your priorities. Don't end up going on a ski holiday when you have just 5K in the bank.

Now, since you want to grow your wealth and you are starting with nothing, essentially, you must learn to trade your labor for big-ticket items like housing and food. For example, take some training classes and become a certified nursing assistant. This would allow you to trade your labor for housing. Find a job taking care of an elderly person at night in exchange for a place to live. You can also become a leasing agent and run a small apartment complex in exchange for housing.

When you first arrive back in Texas, check into a state park. Sleep in your car, and shower there until you find a better situation.

Once your business starts to prosper, pay others to do the physical work, and you complete the mental work. It is wasteful to do physical labor yourself if you can use your intelligence to make more money in the same amount of time.

Always write a contract and sign it with the laborer you are hiring. In America, you must follow contracts.

A problem with having an education and being accustomed to the middle-class lifestyle is that you do not know how to save money. The average American spends huge sums on prepared food, toiletries, and snacks. You need only protein like brown rice and lentils, some greens and fruits. Live very simply and give yourself a treat sometimes. What am I saying? You grew up with Nur as a mother. What a frugal woman she is. No doubt, she taught you how to live for a day on less than the average Westerner spends for coffee.

As you go about your life, please consider these Socratic questions: When is it best to trust, and when is it best to control? In the United States, the federal government gives money to the schools. At the same time, the states make the decisions that run the schools. Many times, the federal government has attached conditions and rules to the monies it gives. Some would say this is an over-reach of control.

You say you want to start a bank. Now is the time to consider these questions because banks are a sore spot in America. Some people say that when Woodrow Wilson created the Federal Reserve, he sealed and doomed the fate of the country. That is a little extreme, but you will need to do a lot of homework if you want to start a bank.

On the other hand, schools in America have been, and are still, guilty of spending money on elective programs other than educating those who need it most—sports over tutoring, computers over literature, gymnasiums over science and math, rich over poor, white over everything. This is not to mention out-and-out instances of graft.

How much incompetence and loss is acceptable in order to preserve freedom from government control? This is a question that will enter your mind thousands of times as you try to buy health insurance on your own terms . . . or not buy it. When you decide to enter the stock market, you may decide to execute your own trades. When you drive a car, buy a house, set up a corporation, hire an employee and so on, this question will enter your mind.

What is the answer? You tell me. You are interested in the moral fiber of the United States, you say. This applies to that, doesn't it? How moral is it to control another person, to invade their domain? Did you like it that I entered your room? How moral is it to act only for one's own benefit at the expense of others? How moral is it to act only for the benefit of others, at the expense of one's own needs? Where does the see-saw stop? Does it ever stop?

We can talk more about morality later. Have you read *Confucius, The Analects*? China was a new grouping of tribes when Confucius and his students created a moral code that allowed each person to govern himself and thus allow society to grow and flourish.

The Ten Commandments are another sort of skeleton that gave many groups the understanding of how to behave toward one another. I could point to other such examples, such as *The Koran* and *The Yoga Sutras*. The point is, when there is no skeleton, no agreement among the poor and the rich alike to follow strict principles of behavior, there can be no capitalism.

I think of the Ten Commandments as a tattered billboard by the highway. We have lost something essential to a strong society—a moral code. In Chicago, they have very strict gun laws, and these laws are ignored. When you try to regulate moral behavior, people will ignore the regulations. Moral behavior must be self-generated.

Capitalism depends on people—on powerful, wealthy business owners—governing their businesses with the same morality that they expect poor workers to apply to their work and home lives. Without this self-governance, Big Government claims justification for its infringement and ultimate dismantling of free enterprise. That is what we are seeing now in the United States, a moral outcry against the excesses of business and the wealthy that will eventually lead to an erosion of freedom. On the other side, we see the grotesque effects of excesses of government: legislators trying to legislate behavior and legislate their own self-interests. Donald Trump? The people who vote for him think they are voting for less government, but they are really voting for less morality, for a bestial society. We are there already in many places, like Chicago and St. Louis.

The people who voted for Bernie Sanders were voting for repression and violence. They don't know this. Only someone who grew up in a Communist society can tell you that the ideals people have about government restraining the excesses of capitalism will dissolve into pools of blood on the pavement: maybe not today, but certainly tomorrow.

Dear Sasha, my son whom I've longed to know, please excuse my speech. For years I've had conversations with you in my head. I was sure when I learned of your existence, that you were my son. I couldn't prove it and I didn't try, but I knew in my heart. Now, my excitement is hard to contain. For you, I know it may be a different story. After all, you have a father, Yusup, whom you grew up with. How I envied him. Whenever you are ready to talk about all of this, I am available.

Until next time, I remain:
Your other father,
Victor
P.S. Good luck.

Sasha slipped the letter into his backpack and sucked air between his teeth. This guy was a badass. He grinned at the thought, "This other father of mine is a badass."

Chapter 3

Remember That Words Are Water

Ambition must be made to counteract ambition.
—James Madison

S ince the underground trains took you straight to Heathrow International, Sasha wouldn't take a bus to the airport. He was packed and waiting on the train platform. He was on his way, after his two-month stay. Although he was not prone to sentimentality, Sasha did call back in his heart to Crandall. He was a friend, after all, and one who had kindly listened to Sasha with sympathy and concern. Well, London wasn't the States. People were less demonstrative here. He hadn't actually said goodbye, but he did have Crandall's address and would send him a letter once he got settled. The man was peculiar about giving out any sort of electronic information. Sasha had actually just copied his address down from the street numbers. "We'll stay in touch," he reassured himself. "He said he wanted a signed copy of my first book. . . ."

The train appeared and Sasha got on, settling in for the ride with his ear buds firmly in place. The ride went smoothly enough. He stepped off the train and began to haul his bags toward the airport entrance when someone lifted the heaviest duffel from behind. He twisted his neck to see Crandall awkwardly trying to help with the load.

"You pack enough clothes?" Although he was tall and stocky, Crandall was pushing 65 and he grunted as he hauled the bag onto his back.

"Hey, thanks for the help," Sasha laughed. "Where'd you come from?"

"Right behind you."

"OK. Well . . . I'm glad you came."

"I couldn't let you leave without saying goodbye."

They marched forward, trading friendly barbs and jokes until they reached the long check-in line.

"This is going to go fast," Crandall nodded toward the line. "These airports have become machines of efficiency." Sasha hadn't told Crandall about Victor because he was unsure whether Victor would want anyone else to know he existed. Still, he wanted to tell Crandall about his "new" father.

"Crandall, I got a letter from a guy who says he's my biological father."

"No way."

"Yes. He said he's my father. Um, he says my mom recently got in touch with him."

"Hmm. That's . . . interesting. . . . What did you say?"

"I didn't have much time. I wrote him back and took the risk of asking him to review my business plan for the next five years or so. He sent me a list of ideas and suggestions right away."

"That's good."

"What do you think about it, about him?"

"Well, I wouldn't know, Sasha." Crandall looked at the fresh, naïve young man before him with kindly concern. "Trust yourself. Just listen to your gut. Pay attention. Maybe this could be a good thing."

"Yeah. I'm just . . . ." Sasha shrugged and grinned and said, "I'm just playing it by ear."

Crandall nodded and opened his arms broadly. "Come here and give me a hug. Don't be shy. I'll show up some day and want a tour of Disneyland. Isn't that what visitors want to do when they come to America?"

Sasha hugged Crandall's broad shoulders. "Yes. Well, Disneyland and Florida. Take it easy, Crandall. Thanks for letting me in at three AM that day."

Crandall tugged on his beard, his eyes watery. "Don't forget to send me an autographed copy of your book when it comes out."

Sasha nodded and said, "You will be the first person." The two men parted, each glad they'd met to say goodbye. Who knew when or if their paths would ever cross again?

The flight was long and cramped. Sasha dozed fitfully, dreaming of trains and buses and lakes and oceans.

Finally, he stood sagging by the curb at the Austin International Airport watching for Julia's silver Prius. He kept a black Nike nylon cap over his head. No need to shock her with his curly red hair just yet.

She showed up as she said she would when he'd texted her, asking for a ride from the airport. Sasha wasn't used to asking for help, but he knew that Julia liked him, so he figured she would come to pick him up, and she did. "Sasha!" she said, her small face shining with delight at seeing him again. Julia was an American of Japanese descent and quite pretty. A lot of the guys had wanted to go out with her, but for some reason, she chose Sasha. He was flattered, but not really interested in more complications in his life at this point. He hoped Julia would be happy just being friends. Yet . . . he knew in his heart that if he really didn't want complications, he could have called Uber for a ride.

This was a tender point with Sasha, the exchange of favors between himself and women. His mother had spoken to him many times about how to treat women. She frankly told him that she wanted to raise a son who behaved differently from his father and did not perpetuate certain harmful ways. She openly admitted that most women would raise their sons to respect women if they could, but tribal customs prevented it in China and neighboring mountain countries. Of course, violence was quickly ruled out for Sasha. The need to speak openly and honestly of one's intentions was another of her strong instructions.

Nur was always doing something else when she spoke with him. He remembered her chopping up a chicken with a cleaver and cutting off its feet for emphasis, saying, "You are making a contract when you speak. Words are water

[chop], they the most powerful force [chop]. Speak your feelings [chop to body cavity]. Don't lie [chop]. Don't hide [chop]."

At the time, he thought her advice was clear and simple. Now that he was parsing his emotions and his desires, he saw that it was not. What if you would lose your chance if you told the truth? He struggled with the fierce competitiveness Yusup had ingrained in him and his mother's equally fierce advice. Certainly, all questions were momentarily shelved for him the minute he saw Julia's beautiful face.

"Where to?" Her silky hair swung against her cheekbones and her eyes sparkled.

Sasha grinned shyly and said, "Oh, just take me to the Red Roof Inn near campus."

"A hotel? You want to go to a hotel?" Her face clouded.

"Yes, please just take me to the Red Roof Inn, Julia. I'm just getting a little rest, and then I'll be flying out again."

He didn't give Julia an opening to ask about his family at this point, and he could see the strain in her face and hear it in her voice as she struggled not to ask. Instead, she said, "Where are you going?"

"I've thought it over and I think the best place for me right now is San Francisco."

"Why San Francisco?" She could not hide her dismay.

"It's by the sea. There is an environmentally conscious population living there. They have a lot of old people and house shares. Also, I like it. I like California.

"I did some research on the various licenses and regulations required to set up a business in California. It's heavily regulated, but I want to start out hard."

"Start out *hard*?"

"Yes. My dad used to always tell me, 'First time, do it the hardest way.'"

Julia nodded and said, "Ah, yes. Like when you solve a math or science problem, the most difficult approach helps to define a more elegant solution later."

He nodded and said, "Yes. Also, a friend of mine gave me the same advice, sort of. He told me to work in my mind to find every single possible way to do something. Compare and weigh money versus time versus public reputation versus expandability. Then, hold it all up to the light of what you know is good and right in the sight of God. If, in the end, you have to lose money or time or even opportunity in order to do the right thing, then lose it. Your spiritual gain is more important, and, eventually, if you keep looking, a new way will open up for you that you did not see before. Never let money hold your conscience ransom, he told me."

Julia remained silent. They had never spoken of their faiths to one another. He didn't know what she believed. When they came to a red light, she turned and looked him in the eyes. "Thank you for telling me your thoughts," she said. "I understand what you mean. I agree with your friend." He could see that she really did understand. She timidly added, "San Francisco is expensive. You could stay in Texas and go to Houston maybe if you want to be by the water." He knew she was asking him to stay.

Sasha smiled at Julia and said, "I could see you more often if I lived in Houston, but I don't like Houston. It's a city that is built on a swamp. Julia, I want to keep talking with you, but I'm not ready to be in a relationship right now. I've lost my family, in a way, and I need some time to deal with that." He reached up and slowly removed his hat. She gasped at the sight of his hair and started to giggle.

"Oh . . . Oh . . ." The light turned green, and she drove silently to the hotel parking lot and turned off the engine. When she turned to look at him, her face was serious in an effort to respect his privacy. She said, "OK. I see, Sasha. We can keep talking. Where are you flying next?"

"I'll buy a car here that conforms to California emissions standards and then drive to 'Frisco." She nodded and smiled an inscrutable smile.

As he opened the door and stood with his bags, she handed him a large white bag. "Here is a Japanese picnic." He took the bag gratefully, glancing at her.

"That was nice of you."

She bowed a little and smiled from the driver's seat. "My pleasure. There is a bus that goes straight to the airport in front of the Administrative Services building on campus."

"Ah. Good to know. Thanks. We'll be in touch. If . . . if you're ever in San Francisco, give me a call," Sasha's body tensed as he said this, but he meant it.

She nodded, waved goodbye, and drove away.

Sasha found dumplings, rice balls, and even a few Chinese delicacies in the bag. As the flavors of home reminded him of his mother, he wondered for the hundredth time where she was and if she was ever going to talk to him again. Part of Sasha wanted to stop right there on the edge of freeway, near his university, where his childhood with Nur and Yusup had been. He fought off the urge to sink into an easy IT job, a convenient apartment, and a lifestyle of Austin coffee house comfort, wrapping himself in the blanket of the past and dreaming of his youth as if he could find it again.

"The beginning is always hard," he reminded himself as he trudged to his room, the setting winter sun a light hand against his back. That was Wednesday. He had $4,650.00 of his $5,000.00 left.

By the time the sun set on Saturday, Sasha was slipping into his sleeping bag in the back seat of his used Toyota. He'd left Austin early Friday morning, after buying and registering the car. He spent the night at a rest stop in the foothills of the Sierra Nevada Mountains. He had $3,000.00 left.

He drove into San Francisco at 3 PM the next day. Excitement shot through his body. This was a new beginning by the sea. The sea spun silver and gray around the city and drew him into its motion. He hoped he could find a place within walking distance of the shore. After buying a big bag of almonds for $10.00 and a bag of apples for $5.00, he drove to the nearest state park and checked in for the night for $25.00. He had to find a Chinese grocery store soon and get some seaweed and rice noodles. Then, he could survive for a week, he estimated, on $30.00 or less.

By midweek, using Craigslist and Care.com, Sasha had interviewed with a man and his daughter, from Singapore, about getting a room in their house in exchange for taking the man to the bathroom at night, administering meds, and helping to bathe him in the evenings. He also agreed to prepare dinner for the man, Al, seven nights a week and do his laundry. He didn't have to get certified to be a nurse's assistant. Normally, the daughter said, she would have preferred that he was certified, but the fact that he spoke her father's language, he was so young and strong-looking, and he had references satisfied her.

The daughter's name was Rose. Rose was very clear that his dinner was not included when he made Al's dinner. He made a note to himself to store all his food in his room, to prevent any misunderstandings. He sighed at the constant attention each tiny step took: inventory, pennies counted, contracts, barters, plans, and regulations. His life would always be like this, only bigger and more. He might as well get used to it.

Rose said to him in a stern voice, "I am busy. I am a mother, a wife, and a daughter. Your help is very important to me. We cannot stay here at night; it is not safe because of the fault. Also, we have young children, and they would disturb him. My father is old, and if he dies in an earthquake, that means his time has come." Sasha looked into her tired eyes and thought, "At least you have a father."

Al's '70s-style house was a split level in Richmond, an hour outside San Francisco to the north. It was half an hour from the ocean and sat on a hill almost exactly over the Hayward Fault line. Sasha was happy to accept the earthquake risk, especially when he found that the basement had an unused kitchen. The daughter had agreed to let him use the kitchen as a lab, provided he was only testing water and not mixing volatile chemicals. He agreed, even though he knew that oxygen was certainly volatile under the right conditions.

Sasha began his new job immediately. He found that Al woke at 12, 3, 5, and 6 in the morning. He had a bell, but to be on the safe side, Sasha moved his bed into Al's room. If Al tried to get out of bed on his own, he would surely fall. Sasha learned to use the oxygen machine, watch the pill count, maintain sanitary procedures, and how to keep Al calm. Al liked to hear about the weather and the fishing conditions in Singapore.

Sasha steadied Al from the back as they moved with the walker toward the bathroom, and in Mandarin, Al recited from memory each day the same thing: "Today, the sun will rise in *Singapore* at 6:57 hours, and sunset will be at 19:07 hours. In the high tide and low tide chart, we can see that the first high tide was at 2:55 hours, and the next high tide will be at 16:15 hours. The first low tide will be at 9:35 hours, and the next low tide at 21:45 hours. Today we will have 12 hours and 10 minutes of sun. The solar transit will be at 13:02 hours. The water level is falling. There are *5 hours and 46 minutes* until *low tide*."

When he was alone, he remembered Victor's advice about written contracts. He found the Richmond library and typed up and printed a contract listing all of his duties and outlining his use of the kitchen downstairs as a lab. When he handed it to Rose, she sat down and wrote on it, "Tenant agrees to unannounced inspections by landlord." She handed it back to him and said, "My husband is a chemist. He will check there is nothing dangerous." Sasha nodded and signed his name next to hers.

Later that night as he lay listening to Al's breathing, he considered the direction he should take going forward. Should he prepare to file business papers once the active water business was up and running? This would require site compliance and probably more taxes than he would be able to pay. Should he run the business as a sole proprietorship for the first year? Was there a middle ground, where he could start a small business and research company without losing his shirt to fees and taxes? He made a note to visit the closest Small Business Administration office the next day, after his job interviews. As he drifted off to sleep, the thought crossed his mind, "What about a partner?"

As Sasha ironed his shirt and tie the next morning, he was grateful for Victor's advice about bartering for living arrangements. It would have been difficult to iron his shirt from his car. He would have been losing precious dollars every day paying rent. He also said a prayer of thanks for Yusup, who had insisted that he pack his suit. He had two interviews today, one with a municipal sewage treatment plant and one with a company that sold water purifiers.

At the sewage treatment plant, the interviewer was an older man wearing an all-khaki uniform. He asked Sasha standard questions about the testing process, went over basic work guidelines, and gave him a tour of the facility. Sasha noticed that the atmosphere was relaxed, and there were dozens of employees moving about the facility. They had their own cafeteria, which served breakfast and lunch. The price for scrambled eggs was $5.00. He shook his head. He would be eligible for full health benefits and a matching 401K for less than 3 percent of his income. He would be a salaried employee—that is, exempt from overtime pay—and expected to work overtime a few times a year. It was a good salary by California standards, $48,000. When Sasha left, he had a feeling that the job was his if he wanted it.

His other interview was at Water Macro, a water-purifying company behind a warehouse on the harbor. The office manager/bookkeeper also acted as the secretary/receptionist. She showed him into a small room with temporary walls. As he waited, he heard the phone ringing, salesmen coming and going, and a secure-area lock being opened and closed. So, they had a secure area, a lab.

After 15 minutes, the door opened and he blinked as two striking women entered, each with platinum blond hair piled on her head in cascades. One woman wore a black jacket and skirt over bulging triceps and thigh muscles. The other woman wore a lab coat that also covered massive musculature. Marlena and Jan had retired, he learned, from the women's wrestling circuit 10 years ago. They had combined their significant winner's earnings and endorsement fees to form this water-purification business. Their primary clients were a psychiatric hospital in San Francisco and a chain of gyms, which they had endorsed in 2011.

They were painstakingly careful to explain to him that he would be a contract employee and responsible for all of his own taxes. He would be expected to work overtime during the summer. His hourly wage would be $28.00, no benefits. His contract would be for 12 months and would be automatically renewed after his yearly review, if all went well. When he said that he was fine with such an arrangement, they stood up and showed him the lab, which was a vast warehouse with lab stations set up every 100 feet. Fifteen technicians were busy testing water to be purified or water that was purified. Marlena pointed to a large wall chart outlining the company's complex process. He recognized the basic procedures in it. Sasha looked into the faces of the technicians around him. They were so intent on their work . . . so intent. He turned to Marlena and Jan and asked, "Do you have a daily test quota you expect each technician to complete?"

"Yes. It's not rigidly enforced, but we do expect you to complete at least twenty-five tests per day."

Sasha nodded. He could certainly do that. Back in the office, Marlena offered him the job. He told the former champion wrestlers that he would let them know the next day, which was Friday.

Friday morning, he sat down with a Small Business Administration advisor and outlined his business plan. After two hours, the advisor printed out a breakdown for him of all expected legal filings, fees, and inspections he would need to complete in order to sell treated water and perform research. Another page showed the set-up costs for patenting and outsourcing manufacturing of an instant test for pharmaceutical contamination on the retail and wholesale markets. Bottom line, the advisor said, "You're either going to need a loan or a partner. Even with robust sales in the water market, you'll fall short two hundred thousand dollars in your first year of operation."

Sasha looked at the numbers, calculating the taxes and noting that he would have to move to an area zoned for industrial manufacturing: his basement lab idea would not work if he wanted to operate a legitimate business. He slipped the pages into his notebook, shook the advisor's hand, and promised to let them know if he wanted to apply for an SBA loan. The advisor assured him that he could qualify for a loan that would cover at least half his shortfall. He wondered if that was wise on the government's part. In fact, he already knew that to access that amount of loan money before he was up and running would only work if he defaulted within the first year. Taking money with no intention of paying it back was dishonest, especially since he was technically robbing himself as a taxpayer.

Things were getting complicated. He repeated to himself, "Start hard. Start hard." Yusup was not there to talk to about this, and neither was Nur or even Victor, Crandall, or . . . Julia.

Sasha took the train into the city botanical gardens and walked among the giant fragrant flowers. In a common area, he sat down on the grass. The jobs were similar, but the city job offered much more health coverage than he could afford on his own. It also gave him a way to save. He knew that he had no choice in terms of the mutual funds the city was using to create his 401K. He also knew that he could not touch the 401K money for quite some time. This was not really the kind of liquid savings he needed as an entrepreneur. He was young, and if he had to buy health insurance by law, he could find some for $100.00 a month. No, the private-industry job was better on paper. He suspected that the water-purifying company job was a stressful one. Nevertheless, he felt that the trade-off of an extra $600.00 in earnings after taxes was worth the risk. After food, gas, and car insurance, registration, and maintenance, he'd have $4,237.00 out of $5,000 per month. If he saved half of that, he'd have about $2,100.00 to use as capital each month. He knew that he could save more than half.

Slowly, Sasha began to formulate an idea. He had to find an established, properly zoned and inspected industrial manufacturing company that would umbrella his venture for a piece of the profits. He needed this kind of partner.

He leaned against a tree and watched a young couple kiss on a blanket nearby. He looked at his phone. He wanted to call Julia . . . someone . . . and tell them what he was thinking. His mother's strict, piercing eyes entered his mind and jarred his impulse to call Julia. He put down his phone. "She's not your psychologist. You want advice, you give love. Every word is a contract. Words are water." In China, water was the strongest force and the most dangerous because it could go around any obstacle, because you could not pull it back, once you let it out, not all the way.

Sasha held back. He closed his eyes and prayed, "Divine Father, Mother, Friend, are you there?" He waited, keeping his mind on God. Slowly, a peace stole over him, and he knew he was not alone. "What should I do?" he asked. For over an hour, Sasha sat still under the tree, keeping his mind focused on God in the way he had learned in meditation. He repeated a mantra to himself: "Be still and know that I am." As the three o'clock hour came and a heavy rain began to fall, he stood up with these words running through his mind and heart, "Flow freely forward."

Chapter 4

Wealth Is a Spiritual Thing

The essence of Government is power; and power, lodged as it must be in human hands, will ever be liable to abuse.
—James Madison

S asha's life was beginning to have a shape. He had accepted the job at Water Macro, the water-purification company. His nights with Al had become familiar. When Al called out in his dreams now, Sasha knew what he was dreaming about: the war, running the farm, the loss of his sister in a flood. Sasha routinely sang a Uyghur child's alphabet song to Al as the old man lay under his oxygen mask and the machine purred on the table beside his bed. Al did not know the Uyghur language, only Mandarin, or mainland, Chinese. Still, Sasha reasoned, he must enjoy hearing a song in the night; Sasha enjoyed singing it.

In this way, he spoke his own language at least once a day. He thought of his mother as he got up and down from his bed throughout the night. When he was a baby, did she have to get up three times a night to feed him? Was his mother a Uyghur, or did she just pretend to be? Was she really a Han Chinese, one of the majority who had tried to kill them and drove them out of China? Then he

39

would stop and shake his head, shake himself. What difference did it make what ethnic group his mother came from? She lived among the "Turkish Chinese" and sang their songs and prayed their prayers. Yet, Sasha was fairly certain that his mother was not actually a Muslim. Very carefully she had taught him to sit still and meditate, using mantras to focus his mind on God. He argued with himself—she knew intricate Uyghur prayers and rituals and ways of dress. Could a spy really learn all of these things? Sasha sighed heavily. He loved the freedom of the United States. Former enemies went to school and worked together. Why fight, especially over religion?

He briefly closed his eyes, remembering his fear as the Han Chinese raided his village when he was nine years old, killing all Muslim Uyghur people. Over a period of three nights, his mother dug a hole in the earth behind their house. She dug it into a steep hillside and away from trails. She used a flat stone to cover the cave-like hole except for a small space. Then, she showed him how to slip into the hiding place and pack earth into the opening so he could not be found. One lazy afternoon as she hung out the wash, he sat nearby translating a poem she had given him.

They heard a scream and a shot. She pointed toward the hiding place, and he ran without looking back. Quickly entering the space, he packed the earth down and added more rocks until it was closed. Next to the wet earth, he heard the raised voices, the calls, the smell of gun smoke. No one came down the steep hill into the thorns and slippery leaves. The riotous crowd stayed close to the road, shooting and killing their Muslim neighbors as they went. His heart beat wildly. Where was his mother? Was she dead, was she wounded? Still, he waited long into the night, crouched in his tiny cave.

At three or four in the morning, he carefully crawled out and up the hill, blindly moving like a snake through the rocks in the dark until his fingers felt a brick wall. Along the wall he crawled, pausing and listening. As he rounded the corner of the house, he saw his mother's body among several others in the street in the predawn light. He ran to it, muffling his cries, which turned to screams as she suddenly laid her hand over his mouth and whispered. "Go hide inside the house, they have already left. Wait for me, I will come to get you. Soon."

He stumbled into their small brick home in the darkness, confused but overwhelmingly happy that his mother was not dead. His father had already left to seek asylum in the United States. He ignored the broken furniture and ransacked rooms. He crawled under the biggest bed and lay there, not daring to sleep. Less than an hour passed before he heard the sound of a car. She came and got him then, and they crawled through a panel in the back seat into the trunk. He lay in her arms while an unknown driver sped away to Turkey. He realized that his mother had pretended to be dead. Even today, Sasha shook his head in disbelief thinking about it. They must have kicked her, thrown knives at her—she was bruised and bloodied. That day haunted him still, and, strangely enough, he had a reminder of its terror the first day he went to work at Water Macro.

It was in the break room during lunch on his first day that he was triggered, tripping into his dark memories. Unlike some companies, everyone ate their lunch at the same time at Water Macro. The low-ceilinged industrial break room with vending machines and folding tables quickly became crowded with water testers unpacking their lunches and chatting with one another. It wasn't until he was sitting down among them, chewing on a rice ball, that Sasha realized that the voices around him were not speaking English. He recognized Chinese, Hungarian, Russian, and . . . Romanian here and there. He turned to the man across from him and asked in English, "Is everyone here an immigrant?" The man, tall, thin, blond, and in his forties, nodded.

"Yes, we are mostly all from somewhere else." He stuck out his bony hand and said, "My name is Daniel. I'm from Romania."

Sasha shook Daniel's hand. "Sasha. I am from China." He had started to say the name of his region, when he caught himself. One of the loudest voices in the room came from a Han Chinese man. He spoke with an accent from western China and laughed in an overly loud way. His voice, the way he yelled coarsely at his companions, carried in it the memory of those other voices. Sasha shivered. He put his hand to his forehead and closed his eyes. Daniel touched his sleeve and pointed to a machine in the corner of the room, saying, "It just serves hot tea. Very good." Sasha nodded and swallowed the fear in his throat. He clenched his teeth and took a deep breath.

Sasha then asked Daniel, "Why are there no people here who were born in the United States? Why are so many from Communist countries?" Daniel nodded. "Yes, you will see. They find we are easier to control, those of us who lived under Communist rule. You will see." Daniel turned his thin face down to look into his lunch of olives, grapes, chicken, and cheese. "You will see."

It wasn't long before Sasha realized what would motivate Marlena and Jan to select only immigrants from Communist countries as their employees. As he worked week after week among them, he found the other employees to be passive, unquestioning, driven to work in excess, and unable to take any risk whatsoever. While Water Macro carefully observed the federal mandates regarding worker breaks, they were rigid about taking any sort of unscheduled break for any reason. No phone calls, no conversations except during lunch. If you had a problem with the work area, you pressed a button to call a technician. After some time, Sasha became uncomfortably aware that many of his co-workers actually wore diapers in case they had to urinate and had already used their break time.

The written contracts for workers stated eight-hour days with occasional overtime. In fact, every worker was expected to work 10 hours every day. Even though they had the right to say no, no one did. Their past experiences in repressive regimes had created in them a *gulag*, or prisoner, mentality. Sasha worked an hour over his shift once or twice a week, but he had to leave to catch the bus back home so he could start his shift with Al. Each time he punched out, he felt the cumulative fear and anxiety of the group. In college, he had studied group mentality, especially its effect in the workplace and productivity. He calculated the increased profits Water Macro was reaping as a result of the extra hours the workforce was putting in—$250,000 per month, or about 12 percent more. He found that while the workers' income went up, so did their taxes, and the income increase wasn't enough to offset their health cost losses and additional childcare expenses.

He had studied the effects of long hours on the working poor in America. As one parent returns home, the other leaves for work, but two incomes and four jobs are often not enough for the basics. When human beings only come home to sleep, relationships simply fall by the wayside. These workers were people, he realized, who had been conditioned to a kind of slavery.

Because of the power of the work culture, Water Macro was definitely benefitting at the expense of their workers. It was far from a fair exchange. Thank goodness for U.S. labor laws; Sasha shuddered to think what Marlena and Jan would attempt if it were not illegal. In China, most workers lived in large compounds. Their rooms were the size of refrigerator boxes. The company officers controlled them, keeping them working, watching their every move. The compounds were massive, gray blocks of human misery. If you made a mistake, if you made a decision that resulted in a failure or loss, you would be fired, and you would not find another job. Fear ran in the workers' veins. They followed, they obeyed.

As the weeks passed, little by little, Sasha gently and carefully asked questions. Gradually, he heard from each person about inefficient methods, incorrect science, and poor customer service. "Why don't you tell someone?" he asked them. Each time, they talked about fear, terrible fear. No.

One older woman from Singapore pointed out with a shrug, "They do not ask me. I do not tell."

After six weeks at Water Macro, Sasha got home one night at 7 PM, 30 minutes after his shift with Al started. He rushed in the door, throwing his backpack on the floor. "I'm so sorry, Karen," he started to say to the day nurse, but his words froze in his mouth. The woman feeding Al his dinner was not Karen. She looked up calmly, her green eyes flashing at him, a wide smile on her wide face.

"No problem. You're Sasha? I'm Suki. I'm subbing in for Karen this week. Her son is getting married."

Sasha nodded and said, "Right. She mentioned you to me. I just thought it was next week." Sasha was surprised that Rose had OK'd Suki. After all, didn't she want someone who could communicate with her father? Suki was an extremely round, compact black woman with a streak of pink on one side of her hair and a streak of purple on the other. She had jewelry peeking from many piercings on her dark brown nose and ears. She reminded Sasha of a sumo wrestler or Mulan, the Mongolian Disney princess.

He bent down next to Al and asked him in Chinese how he liked this new woman. Al smiled, nodded, and said, "Zhè me piào liang de wēn nuǎn de shǒu kě ' ài de gū niang." ("So nice. Warm hands. Sweet girl.")

Suki nodded, bowed, and said, "Thank you for your kind words," in perfect Mandarin. Sasha blinked. "Ha, ha! You should see your face. You didn't think I could speak Chinese?" Suki let him off the hook. "That's OK. I'm from Korea, but I also speak Chinese and Japanese."

Sasha nodded. He knew that there was a small black population in Korea. Still, she didn't have a Korean accent. He ventured a statement: "You have an American accent."

Suki's green eyes were distracting. He stared at them without realizing it. Suki pretended not to notice and said, "I'm adopted. I came here when I was about ten. Who knows where my green eyes come from. I figure a GI or maybe a Russian. You know, Russian women were once rulers in Egypt. They were brought over as slaves and eventually rose to be the wives of Pharaohs."

Sasha had already taken over feeding Al. He felt an electrical jolt hit his heart and explode. Was he really so lonely, so isolated that meeting an Asian woman his own age with a similar sort of physical trait as his red hair would cause him to turn inside out? The answer was yes. YES. Sasha turned to face her and took off his hat. His orange 'fro popped out.

"Oh, wow," Suki said, hopping up and clapping her hands. She turned to Al and asked, "Al, did you know your boy had red hair?" Al was actually laughing. Sasha had never seen him laugh out loud. He had big teeth.

Suki gathered up her things. "Hey, I've got to go. I'll see you tomorrow?" she said. Sasha smiled. "Sure. I'll see you then," he said. After she'd left, Sasha shook his head in amazement. What had just happened? It couldn't be romantic attraction; he was attracted to girls who looked like Julia. No, this could be the beginning of a friendship. He tried not to feel desperate. He tried to be super laid back.

In the days that followed, Sasha made sure to leave work in time to spend an extra 30 minutes with Suki before she left Al in his hands. On Thursday, he asked her if she'd like to hang out on the weekend, maybe go check out some music in the park. Most of the workers at Water Macro came in on Saturdays and Sundays. Sasha did show up at work two weekends a month, just to keep the Water Macro management spotlight off him.

This Saturday, he left at noon and went home to change. He'd learned that Suki loved jazz, danced really well, and could sing a haunting version of any country western song in Korean. She was one of the warmest, funniest people he had ever met. Being with Suki was, Sasha thought, the same feeling as being in front of Crandall's fireplace while he read Sasha's poems. Suki felt like home to him.

He grinned as he got ready. He had five hours before he had to be back. Most caregivers either worked weekdays or weekends, but Sasha worked both in order to keep his room. Every Saturday and Sunday night found him with Al. This was the first Saturday that he wished he didn't have to be back so soon.

They met at the park and walked to a spot in front of the stage. Suki spotted people she knew, and she introduced him to everyone as her co-worker. She laid out a blanket for them to sit on and then left, coming back with a very pregnant woman and her three young children. "Hey, Sasha, can we fit Blanca's kids on this blanket? She's gotta go have her baby all of a sudden, and I sort of offered." Sasha could see that Blanca was straining with a labor pains, and her legs were dripping wet.

"Yes, of course." He quickly scooted to the edge and patted the center of the blanket. Blanca spoke in a kind but commanding voice to her two girls and one boy in Spanish. She smiled thanks to Sasha and Suki and then waddled off to a beat-up Ford van, where her husband had made a pallet in the back. She got in, and he skidded off.

As the evening wore on, Sasha helped Suki with the kids and didn't get to listen to much music or talk to Suki. He did learn that she knew Blanca from volunteering with a group called Christos. As the band wound down, he helped her load the kids into her car. She related to them in a quiet, calm way that belied her colorful appearance. At 11 that night, she called him. "Hey, thanks for being so supportive today," she whispered. "Blanca had another boy. The kids are staying with me."

Something had been nagging at him all night, so he asked her, "Are you a Christian, like an evangelical Christian?" His heart pounded. He'd heard stories about these evangelical Christians in America. What if his great, new friend was one of them?

"Yes. Well, I'm not rabid and or crazy, if that's what you're afraid of, but yes, I am a Christian in that I follow Jesus Christ and his teachings. I was raised by missionaries, so, naturally I rejected Christianity for a while. But eventually, after reading about and trying a few other things, I really felt as I prayed and asked for guidance . . . I felt like Jesus Christ showed up with this huge outpouring of love for me. . . . What can you say to love like that except, 'I love You back'?" She paused, then said, "As for 'evangelical,' no. I think that if you're walking the spiritual path, that's going to call attention to your beliefs right there because it's quite different from the norm. So, no, I don't spend time telling other people that their faith is bogus and mine is the only way." She chuckled good-naturedly.

Sasha smiled on his end but didn't say anything. An easy silence hung between them. "OK, well . . . ," Sasha coughed. "You know, Suki, I don't know anyone who is as comfortable with herself as you are. You laugh so often and smile so much that everyone wants to be around you, including me. If Jesus Christ has impressed you this much, then that is something I have to respect . . . and envy," he added.

Even though she hadn't told him, Sasha knew that Suki had had her struggles with her family in Minnesota and with attitudes in general toward her as a black person and as an intellectual female. She had even caused a big commotion with her family when she dropped out of medical school to study art. "Thank you, Sasha. I appreciate you being so open. I really do. Maybe we can try again at the park next Saturday. I don't have any other friends who are ready to drop their babies." She laughed then. It was a long, free-flying, joyous laugh that was almost a song.

"I'm planning on it," Sasha assured her. They said goodnight. "It's great to have a sister," he thought as he dropped down on his bed to read some poetry before he had to walk Al at midnight. As he opened his dog-eared book of haikus, a folded letter fell out. He stared at it, his stomach tightening in excitement. Shades of Putney Bridge bus! Victor, you old rascal. He was glad to know that Victor had somehow found him.

Sasha's fingers trembled slightly as he opened the letter. It was indeed from Victor. "That guy gets around," he mused as he counted the pages, three. Ah, a nice long letter.

Dear Sasha,

I told you I am your father, and I am. I feel that I owe you some more information about myself. You were in a hurry to start a new life during our last correspondence. Now that you're more settled and on your way, maybe we can get to know one another.

First, let me give you some information about your mother. I believe that she is alive and well and will get in touch with you when she is ready. I know this about Bo, or as you call her, Nur. Actually, it could be that her name is Bo Nur, or Precious Light. Bo Nur told me that she was born into a small village in the foothills of the mountains to a Uyghur family. When she was four years old, her mother got a letter in the mail from her family about a hundred miles away. They told her of a raging illness that was killing many people, especially women and children. It might have been scarlet fever or smallpox or bird flu. She didn't tell me. Out there, it could have even been typhoid. Her mother had a newborn, a two-year old son, and Bo Nur was her oldest. She said that right after she got the letter, her mother dressed her up in all of her clothes, layer after layer, until she could barely walk. Then her father put her on his donkey and they traveled up the mountain for four days to a small cabin in a small valley where a hermit lived. He was actually an Indian yogi who had somehow found his way to a cave in the snowy peaks bordering western China. Her father put her on the donkey and sent it walking up to the man's door and . . . he ran the other way.

She told me that her father must have been afraid that the old yogi would refuse to take her, which was very likely. The long-haired Vedic came out to find a little girl on a donkey. He was kind to her and gave her some goat milk and little red berries he had harvested. She stayed with the man, Babama, on the mountain for a year. He sang her songs in Hindi and taught her to meditate.

When she turned five, he took her into a very small gathering high in the mountains where the children went to school out-of-doors. Babama was actually an educated man, and he stayed and became the teacher for the group of about six families. They built him a house, and he raised Nur with help from the village. He was not a Uyghur; he taught her many different ways of thinking.

When she came of age, she won a scholarship to a college in Beijing. Somehow, at the university, she ended up being arrested during a protest. They were about to put her in prison for a long time, when they realized that she spoke seven or eight languages. That's how she became a security services person, a spy. She had no choice. I'm sure there's more to it, but you will have to ask her the next time you see her. The reason I fell in love with Nur was because she was so very honest and fierce. I never met anyone with her integrity and courage. I was used to long-legged blond beauties, and Nur was this tiny, quiet and sort of argumentative woman. She was a far better spy than I. I could have resented her, but when we got to know one another, when she explained to me why she did what she did, her reasons were based on her desire to please God, to do the right thing wherever she was. After a while, I loved her. It wasn't a love that came from sexual attraction, it came from . . . well . . . just this deep love that she awakened in me. That's all I can say about it. It's still a mystery to me. I never loved anyone else. After she left, I went to Switzerland, and after that, well, I just didn't want to be with anyone else.

Now, about me: I was born with a head of rust-colored hair. My mother was a strawberry blond, and my father had dark red hair, too. Lucky me! In Russia, many people have red hair, so I did not really stand out. I was a wiry boy who liked to climb everything. I got into trouble for climbing neighbors' trees, walls, sides of trucks and even ropes at the harbor. I loved climbing so much that I would sneak around trying to find new and exciting things to climb. I don't know why I liked it so much, but finally, my father drove me 200 miles to the mountains. Here, he hired a man to teach us both how to rappel down the side of a cliff. I loved it. I worked and saved my money and took many trips back to those *mountains. I became one of the best mountain climbers in Russia by the time I was 17. When I was 18, that's when they "recruited" me into the secret service. Well, my father was a member of the Communist Party. He was an accountant for a large company that built apartment buildings. When I was ready to go to university, my father encouraged me to join the security forces and let my studies be guided by my job requirements. It made sense at the time. I studied languages and finance, and you know the rest.*

That's a little about me. My mother and father, your grandparents, are no longer living. They died within weeks of one another, of cancer. I have one sister, and she lives in Rustove-on-Don, a city in the south of Russia. She really enjoys running her own restaurant there. Her name is Katia. My full name is Victor Sasha Mikel Tishvosky. Obviously, you are named after me. The name Sasha means "little prince."

Sasha let the letter fall. So, she had known all along! His mother had always known he was not Yusup's biological son. He continued reading.

You know that I "retired" from the secret service. Retirement was not easy, since it usually is followed by an early and unexplained death. Both your mother and I took advantage of the changes in government that allowed us to slip between the cracks. She was assigned to the Uyghur region and then was able to flee China because of ethnic cleansing. I was so new when I dropped out of sight, I did not pose a threat.

I was living in different parts of Europe for a long time, a year or so in Germany, a year or so in Belgium, London etc. Finally, I settled here in the United States. Eventually, I became a financial advisor, a business owner, and an author. I publish my books under an assumed name. I write about politics, naturally, and also investing and running a business, things like that. I live relatively near you in Washington State. I have to say, I am still getting used to this country. On the one hand, I am thrilled at the power and energy the people have in terms of building new ventures. It's wonderful, really wonderful to be a part of this magnetic nation.

On the other hand, I'm constantly struggling against government regulations that censor my free speech. As a financial advisor, I'm forbidden to say this and I can't say that. It's Big Brother watching over my shoulder just like at the Kremlin. Literally, everything I do as a business owner is circumscribed by the government: employee pay, advertising, firing and hiring, what I pay myself, how I reward my salespeople, how I grow and how much—anti-trust, anti-monopoly, anti-fraud, anti-discrimination. The regulations the Department of Labor issued under the Dodd-Frank law have put a limit on the amount of incentives I can receive or offer any salespeople working for me.

Dear Sasha, I must sound ungrateful and bitter, but what I might sound like and what I really am are two different things. What I really am is an informed, educated citizen who is making his voice heard one way or another. That's why I write books. Your mother used to call me a crazy idealist. She warned me many times that I would endanger myself by speaking up. "I'm not a Communist," I'd tell her. "Not in my heart. In my heart, I'm a free citizen of a capitalistic democracy and I'm going to act like one."

"You and your heart live in different countries," she said to me. That is true. Nur had a way of saying the truth. If you truly believe in free enterprise and democracy, then that belief is a separate country from the one you live in, no matter where you live, even if it's the United States. Even here, I must keep my belief pure, and I must fight for it against the encroachment of government. That's my job. It's my duty.

In fact, Sasha, I believe that those of us who call ourselves conservatives are at a crossroads. We are faced with Donald Trump. Trump is one of the most flawed candidates we have ever had. He is, however, a mirror image of Barack Obama and what one would expect. We have endured Barack Obama and the many restrictions he has placed on the free-market economy. The Affordable Care Act solution is just one of many ways that Obama has hobbled this country. He put so many restrictions on buying and selling mortgage shares, it's difficult to make money. Where we desperately needed people to become more educated and responsible about their spending—look at these oil industry workers who are defaulting on debts—we have instead gained more and more bureaucracy. I hate it. It smells like the place I left, a big, engorged government system that was corrupt and accomplished nothing except repression.

When I read about the Marxist professors in American colleges being allowed full exposure to naïve students, filling them up with propaganda, I feel sick. These kids have had everything. They don't know what they are losing, they don't know what life can be like when you try to control the forces of commerce too much. They don't realize that once you cross a certain line, once you cede a certain amount of control to the government, the government becomes violent. Communism lost its credibility in China when citizens were tortured, disappeared, and massacred. Violence is the face of big government. Tell that to those crowds of young people in Oregon cheering on Bernie Sanders.

I want to start a new coalition of people who have the expertise to create free-market economy solutions to problems that everyday people face, like healthcare and food scarcity, like buying a house. If we'd been there and come up with a truly viable way for working class people to purchase a home, maybe Fannie Mae and Freddie Mac wouldn't have been created and we wouldn't have gone down that dark tunnel into a recession.

Today, we're looking at a 1.5% growth rate after a serious recession. Usually, the growth rate after a recession is around 4%. This sluggish growth is a consequence of over-regulation by the government. The Obama Administration generated over 80,000 pages of new government regulations in a year. It has been more than seven years since wages went up significantly. We are facing complex issues in our economy that cannot be fixed with policy alone or with business alone. We struggle, we struggle to start businesses, to run businesses, to address poverty issues and to communicate honestly with one another. There has to be a working together of these two forces and soon, because we are slip, slip, slipping away.

Conservatives have not been known for stepping up to deal with poverty issues in the past, and I think now is the time for us to do so. We must be proactive before the cries of suffering prompt more policy and laws and government welfare and so forth. Sasha, Venezuela can't even afford to buy and sell beer. Imagine an entire country that can't even afford to buy beer. That's what socialism led to, a lack of buying power . . . pervasive poverty. If we want to avoid losing everything we have in the United States, we've got to find a way to address the concerns of those who work in the trenches of our economy with solutions that draw upon capitalism, not government.

People are souls inside of bodies, Sasha. As souls, they are not bad. As souls, they are perfect reflections of God. They do bad things sometimes because they are ignorant. I'm not at all convinced that making laws about what people cannot do is the best way for them to learn what is right. Call me Libertarian-ish, but I have to tell you, I am engaged in an ongoing swordfight with blundering, aggressive, wrong-minded federal regulations. I build wealth for myself and others despite the United States government.

Wealth: let's cut to the chase. Wealth, for me, is a spiritual thing. I don't mean that I worship money. What I mean is that money doesn't equal wealth. My wealth is not my money. As a person with a large income, I give my money away to charities consistently and conscientiously. This is also part of my job as a citizen. If I am fortunate enough to earn more than I need, I pass a large part of it on to organizations that can assist with education, jobs and health. Nothing is as black and white as it seems, is it? The wealthy support vast networks of charitable works; they also pay large tax bills. Some people say their tax bills should be larger. Why? Why not allow the rich to continue to invest in free enterprise rather than siphoning their money off to feed an insatiable government complex?

While I was holed up in that mountain cave all those years ago, I read hundreds of books. Sometimes I wish I was back there sipping goat milk and turning pages by candlelight. One book I read at least 20 times was the Bible. Intellectually, it had its low points and high points, but what I found as I read the words of Jesus Christ was a great sense of peace. I needed peace. I actually just read His words over and over again because they had a kind of supernatural or subconscious effect of calming me down and helping me to feel safe. "The kingdom of God is within you." "Seek ye first the kingdom of God and all these things will be added unto you."

It wasn't until the thirtieth reading or so of the New Testament that I literally stopped and allowed myself to believe. I say "believe" but that sounds like I became convinced intellectually. That did happen, too, but what I mean when I say "believe" is "experience." I experienced a presence. . . . That's all I can tell you. It was a wave of love so warm and big and real that I could only receive it gratefully. It was Jesus Christ, I'm certain of that. He gave his life for me, and I felt His presence with me. That's all I'm going to say on the matter, unless you bring it up. I just wanted to share that with you since my decision to follow Christ altered my life so drastically.

You probably couldn't tell from the outside that I had been transformed. When I was free to leave Switzerland, I got a job, made friends and kept on living my life, but inside, I was a different person. Everything I said and did from that point on was motivated by a desire to keep and maintain my closeness with Jesus Christ. That became my yardstick instead of status, safety or power. I just wanted that . . . I still do.

Now, Sasha, I want to hear all about what is going on with you. Please write back to me as soon as you can and tell me how you are progressing in your plan. Let me know if you think I can answer any questions or share any knowledge. Here are some questions I have: How are your experiments progressing? What does your research tell you about marketing such an invention as a pharmaceutical-content water test? How can it be the most universally useful?

Yours truly,

Victor

Sasha squinted his eyes in the dimly lit room and laid the letter down. This was an odd coincidence. Here, two people, two friends, had just described a wave of love entering their lives and giving that love a name: Jesus Christ. Strange.

Al began to try to climb out of bed. Sasha jumped up and was at his side in an instant. As he lifted the old man in his arms, he sang the alphabet song and gently lowered his feet to the floor so that he could walk with his walker to the bathroom. Sasha's mind was both calm and busy. He wondered what Victor would say about the way Marlena and Jan treated the Water Macro employees.

If he hated government interference so much, how would he respond to such ridiculous treatment?

He suspected he knew, but he would hurry and write back to find out.

Chapter 5

Create a Collaborative Culture at Work

If men were angels, no government would be necessary.
—James Madison

Sasha could not fall asleep after reading Victor's letter. He went over Victor's description of his mother's childhood again and again. He hadn't said so, but her whole family must have perished during the epidemic. He wondered why they hadn't all come up the mountain together. Why had they stayed behind if they knew they might die? What was the complex social balance sheet that made it OK to save the life of one child but not that of the whole family?

He already knew the answer to that question in the back of his mind; he just didn't want to acknowledge it. They could not forsake their group in a time of crisis. It simply was not in their cultural training to abandon their community in order to save themselves. In China, the individual is only useful as part of the whole. The whole gives the individual purpose and meaning. He realized that the effort to preserve the life of a girl, that in itself was singular. What inner conflicts Nur must have faced as she grew up a strong and independent woman with a mind of her own. Her position as his mother and Yusup's wife had been both real and fake. He wondered if she finally felt free to be herself, now that she was out of China and divorced: "freedom from the oppression of tyranny," isn't that what the Constitution promises U.S. citizens?

Then, there was the news that Victor actually lived a few hundred miles away from him. Victor's honesty about his faith and his business opened Sasha's eyes to a totally different way of life. Growing up as a refugee had meant growing up with Scarcity pounding on the door, real and imagined. Life was to be survived, not created. Victor stood over his choices, observed them, and connected them to his spiritual values.

Sasha had grown up watching circumstances determine his choices for him, for the most part. He did not consider solving problems on a large scale because he was programmed to work for his own family's success and none other. He himself was a kind of human savings account for the family. He even thought of himself, literally, as a human dividend. The passivity that often came with a survival mentality reduced him to a narcissistic machine. His civic duties were narrowly defined by his own interests, so they were not civic duties at all but strategies to achieve greater financial gain. In the Asian community he had been a part of in Austin, the adults gathered to discuss which candidate would be the best for their business profits. No one had ever mentioned ethics, creative and compassionate ways to address poverty, or the dismantling of democracy by special interests. Much conversation went into where to move in the city or the country in order to have access to the best public schools. They were bargain hunters and bargainers, not reformers.

As he lay in bed that night, Sasha pondered the broader and more liberating way that Victor lived and thought. That broad overview was what he wanted. How would his journey into free enterprise be affected if his first guiding principle was "Love your neighbor as yourself," and his second was "Buy low, sell high"? If he was going to be a successful businessman and American citizen, he would have to step outside the box, grab the lines that defined the box, and bend the lines into a new shape. He would have to become a long-term investor in the social and moral fabric of the USA, not just its economy.

At six o'clock in the morning, he got up and walked Al into the shower. At seven o'clock, the day attendant came in, and he was free to do as he wished. He made his way downstairs to the second kitchen overlooking a patio. He still marveled at how enormous this house was: five bedrooms and five bathrooms upstairs, three bedrooms and two bathrooms downstairs. The third level was a small apartment. The living areas were sweeping, oval-shaped rooms, furnished with round couches, lacquered tables, pianos, and rugs. He noticed that all the artwork had been removed. The house was a mystery he hadn't had the time to solve. There was just too much to do. In particular, he needed to start his own experiments. Water Macro didn't seem to be a hospitable "umbrella." For the time being, he would just have to work on his own and play it by ear.

Sasha spent four hours sterilizing the small kitchen, making a list of hoses, gas tanks, pumps, chambers, and filters he would need. He figured that outfitting the lab would cost him about a thousand dollars. It took him another hour or so to calculate and recalculate the fees involved in becoming an established manufacturer. He finally had to put his plans aside and go for a walk.

Walking up the steep hill that ran almost parallel to the Hayward Fault, he forced himself to look at the tops of the trees and recite poetry. He wanted to refresh his mind. The walk was bracing as the cold air from the sea found its way through his cotton shirt and pants. Ahead was a beautiful, white church that had been emptied and was awaiting deconstruction as people tried to salvage the materials. He walked into a splendid mosaic courtyard and through an archway into a private nook with a bench he thought was just right for contemplation.

Sasha sat looking into the center of a pink hibiscus flower. He could almost hear the roar—the roar of life that powered all things and connected them to one another. His mother had told him to listen to the roar, that it was the *Om* or, as the Christians called it, the Holy Spirit. Each leaf that fell, fell in the right way. Each tiny drop of life, each branch and feather grew exactly right. He felt the anxiety drain from his body. He closed his eyes, composing in his mind what he would write to Victor. Soon his thoughts drifted into the sound of the wind. There was such a strong vibration in this place, he felt lifted into a lightheartedness he had not felt since he was a child.

Sasha began to pray. First, he prayed the prayer his mother had taught him as a child: "Oh Beloved God, Divine Mother, Heavenly Father, Friend. Saints and sages of all religions, I bow to you now. I will think, I will will, I will act. Guide Thou my thoughts, my will, and my actions, and may Thy love shine forever on the sanctuary of my devotion, and may I be able to awaken Thy love in all hearts."

Then, he prayed the prayer that Yusup had taught him: "Glory be to my Lord, the Almighty."

He prayed the prayer that Suki had taught him: "Dear God, create in me a clean heart. Lead me in the paths of righteousness for Thy name's sake. Thank you for sending Your Son Jesus to redeem me. Guide me all the days of my life, that I might love my brother as myself and do good unto them that despise me. In Jesus' Name, amen."

Finally, in the deep stillness, he listened for a long time, focusing his attention at the point between the eyebrows, the seat of spiritual consciousness, and silently whispering, "I love You, God." Like an opening rose, joy entered into his consciousness, and he knew that this, this joy, was the treasure of his life.

The shadows in the courtyard lengthened, and Sasha realized that he had to return. He stood up slowly, hating to leave his little sanctuary.

He walked back to the house, opening the giant round doors to slip through the vast living room as he always did and go into his own room. He stopped then and just stood in the center of the room. He looked at the eight 11-foot-tall windows that followed the curve of the oval wall and filtered sunlight with huge swaths of synthetic yellow silk with borders of painted pandas and lanterns. The long sofas were a muted pink, and the rugs picked up this color in giant woven cherry blossoms against a light green and gold wool. The room held a secret, but what was it? It seemed to Sasha that everywhere he went, he stood on the edge of an understanding. Something, something was dawning in his consciousness, but it had not yet shown itself to him.

In his room, he took out a pen and paper and began to write:

Dear Victor,

I cannot tell you how happy I was to receive your letter—albeit an unusual delivery method. I assume I am to leave this reply in the pages of my haiku book? Are we using this method to exchange letters because you do not trust me yet with your address? I hope you can trust me someday, Victor. I believe that you are my father, and I would like to meet you someday.

Thank you for giving me more information about my mother. It will take me a while to fit these pieces together with the woman I knew for so long. I often think of her, and long to see her again. This is something we have in common, isn't it? We love the same woman very much. Where is she? When will I see her again? I ask myself these questions all the time. The Sasha I am today is not the Sasha I used to be. I'm much quieter now. I miss being part of a family. One day, we were all together and we loved each other . . . I thought. The next day, I stood alone. It is difficult for me to understand. Somewhere inside of me, I am waiting to see my mother again and talk to her about all of these things.

I am also grateful to learn more about you. We share a love of mountain climbing. Perhaps you could send me a picture of yourself when you were younger? Do you still have red hair?

I have to admit, Victor, your way of looking at the world is different from mine. I have grown up thinking only of myself and my family. How I could influence the world or what my role as a citizen is did not really cross my mind. I was busy thinking of good grades, a good job, and pleasing my parents. I did study Third World economies and even assisted in teaching some classes about microeconomics. That being said, I never actually considered creating solutions, real solutions to address the problems of Western poverty and American economic weaknesses. Your idea of a coalition is intriguing. When minds come together to brainstorm, there is hope, I think, for a better tomorrow. I'm going to do some research on the topic and come back to you with some questions.

You asked me how I am doing. My answer is that I am doing great. That is not to say that I have had a scientific breakthrough or a business *success. I have made some friends, found a job and started saving money. I went by the Small Business Administration and got a good idea of what my fees and overhead costs would be if I were to start a lab and manufacturing business using my own facility. I'm looking at about $6,000 to $10,000, and that is not including equipment, rent, or operating expenses. I'm able to save $2,500 a month, so if I include a safety plan of three months of living expenses, I will have $8,000 to spend on a new business in less than a year. I suspect I will need more money than I can anticipate, however, especially for insurance.*

I had toyed with the idea of going in under the umbrella of an existing industrial chemical manufacturer and agreeing to cut them in a percentage. I'm actually working at a water-purifying company called Water Macro; it is not going so well there, though, and I'm reluctant to form a business relationship with them.

Here's the problem: The business owners have chosen to hire only people who originally lived in Communist or totalitarian political regimes. They exploit these people's fear of going against authority. The work culture is to work 10-hour days and every weekend. We are all on contract and pay our own taxes. We do not get paid overtime. The way that the work environment is structured does not allow for any feedback or new ideas. In fact, we are treated as a sort of slave group and not even allowed to talk or go to the bathroom except at break times. There are many problems with the processes they are using and with their level of customer service, but none of the employees speak up. I find it very frustrating. I do not work the same hours as everyone else; I leave at the end of an eight-hour shift. These owners seem well-intentioned, but they are not aware.

I was thinking of quitting and going to work at the city lab. One of my co-workers told me that he worked at the city water-testing lab for two years and had almost nothing to do. They hired him to increase his manager's salary. He was so bored, he quit. I, on the other hand, could use the free time to conduct my own experiments. The only problem with that is that I believe I would have to sign an agreement relinquishing all intellectual property before coming on. . . .

In light of the problems at Water Macro, I've prepared as a lab one of the unused kitchens in the house where I live. I expect to have it set up and operational next week. I've already made quite a few process notes, so it's just a matter of testing.

These are some things happening in my world.

The house where I live and work as a caretaker sits right on top of the Hayward Fault. The house is rather strange. I mean, it feels like an Oriental palace. It has an ancient feel to it, as if someone held court there. I wish I knew its history. It is at least 20,000 square feet and three levels. I realize that it is actually a huge financial problem for the owners since they cannot sell it and won't live here because they have young children. Its only occupant is the old father, Aloysius. This is the name the Catholic nuns in Singapore gave him. His Chinese name is Chen-Ze.

I am up about four times a night to take Al to the bathroom. It hasn't bothered me so far. He speaks Mandarin and has told me many stories. He is not a good listener because he is so deaf and forgetful.

My London friend, Crandall, is a good listener. He is an older businessman. I've really missed his company. He used to give me a cup of tea by the fire in the wee hours and read my poetry. That reminds me, I have submitted my book of poems to the grant administrators, and they have graciously published it for me. It will be out next month. If you send me your address, I will mail you a copy. I know that the US mail may seem low level to you, since you have a network of message carriers all your own, but I thought I would mention it. LOL.

I have left out one of the best parts of my life so far, and that is my new friend, Suki. I met Suki because she was subbing as a nurse assistant with my patient one week. Suki is a black woman from Korea. She has green eyes and a snappy personality. She came to the US when she was 10 and was adopted by missionaries in Minnesota. We have hit it off and become friends. I'm going to hear some music in the park with her this weekend. Like you, Victor, Suki is a Christian. She spoke of her experience with Jesus Christ in much the same way you did. I have felt your deep devotion and it has touched me. I feel so fortunate to have found three people I like and trust in such a short period of time.

I hope to hear from you soon. What do you think of my decision to begin testing on my own? I cannot legally manufacture here, so it is a short-term solution to simply invent.
My warm wishes and friendship,
Sasha

Carefully folding his letter, he placed it between the pages of his haiku book and went to sleep. He woke up just in time to get Al's dinner ready. As he was cutting up Al's fish, Rose stuck her head into the dining room. "Hi there," she spoke in Chinese. "How are you guys doing?"

Sasha smiled without moving from his task. "We are fine. He has a good appetite today."

"Yes. Good." Rose sat down next to her father. "How are you feeling, Daddy?"

"I'm feeling very well," Al spoke in a matter-of-fact way as he took another bite. Rose leaned back in her chair and watched her father finish his meal. Sasha didn't want to disturb her while she was visiting her father.

He worked quietly in the kitchen as they chatted. Just as she stood up holding her purse, kissed him goodbye, and was moving toward the door, Sasha managed to hurriedly mention to her that he was going ahead with using the downstairs kitchen as a lab.

She nodded, "OK, well, no explosions."

He nodded also, but he knew there would be small explosions from time to time. Hopefully, none that caused damage or disturbed anyone.

She had her hand on the knob when he ventured to ask, "Rose . . . did you . . . did you and your family live in this house when you were growing up?"

She laughed and said, "Oh no. No, we lived in a small house, a little blue house far away from here on the other side of San Francisco. Our whole house was as big as this living room." She gestured toward the great room.

Her mouth moved slightly from its usual thin line. He thought she was going to smile, but she stopped it halfway. "This house used to belong to my uncle, Uncle Joe. He left it to my parents in his will. When he and his wife came to the United States, they had lost everything. My dad let them take over one of his bakeries. He had two. Uncle Joe and Aunt Amy lived in the back of the bakery for five years. After that time, they were able to buy the bakery from my father. They started making sandwiches and selling coffee and turned it into a little restaurant. It was such a sort of artistic little bakery-café that a film crew shot some scenes from a movie there. They sold the bakery after it was very popular, and they started selling houses. They both got real estate licenses. He became a very successful man . . . again. He had owned most of the land in his province in China before the revolution. He lost it all and escaped to Thailand. He started over and owned a hotel near the water. Before long, he owned three hotels. Sadly, when the tsunami came through, he lost them all. By the time they came to the United States, they were pushing sixty. Still, he began a real estate career and turned over almost twenty houses every six months.

"Uncle Joe and Aunt Amy used to host music parties here with violins and cellos. They made friends with many musicians from China. They tried to get my dad to move his entire family onto the second floor, but my parents refused, for some reason. I was still a child then, so they didn't ask my opinion. I would have loved to live in this house. It's like a palace, isn't it?"

"Yes," Sasha agreed. "It's a remarkable space. What will happen to it?"

She shrugged. "We will probably abandon it someday. The city will take it over."

Sasha nodded. "Oh. Hmmm . . . ." He stood up to walk with Al into the bedroom, and Rose waved as she left.

The next morning when Sasha went into his room to get ready to meet Suki at the park, he saw something lying on his desk. It was an old photograph of a thin, young man with red hair in a green sweater vest. He was pointing to a sign and smiling. The sign had a drawing of a dancing bear on it, and the word "circus" in Russian. Victor: Victor—his father—was standing in front of him. He turned the picture over and saw "1983" written lightly in pencil. He, Sasha, was born in 1991, so this was long before . . . . Victor must have been about 19 years old, a new college student. Sasha stared at the picture, placing it in his framework for Victor's life. There in the background was a light-green

VAZ-2105, a Russian-made car he had often seen when he lived in the Xinjiang Uyghur region bordering Russia.

Sasha blinked. He felt a wave of fear wash over him, and he smelled something. Was it a memory? He couldn't name . . . exhaust? Diesel exhaust? He shook his head. What was that memory? Had he . . . had he actually met Victor once before? Who was driving the car that took his mother and him to safety? He tried to remember. He had fallen asleep. Then, his mother and a man carried him to a bed. When he woke, they were talking quietly in the room. The man . . . he never saw his face, but he did see his car out the window as he drove away. . . . Sasha looked at the photograph again. It could be. It could be.

He put the picture inside his haiku book on the desk and took out the letter he knew was there: thick and reassuring.

Without opening it, he put it in his backpack . He had to go now to see Suki. He would read the letter later.

Sasha rode the bus and then the train over to the beautiful San Francisco Botanical Garden. He loved coming into the city on Sundays. San Francisco on Sundays with a friend in the park— his heart sang with happiness: finally, a respite from work and worry. There she was, standing by a bench and talking to a passerby with a dog. Suki never met a stranger. That day was the best day of his life, Sasha would say in the years to come. They didn't do anything special, just walked and talked and sat down to eat sandwiches. She left to investigate a festival nearby, and he lay down on the grass and watched people playing soccer. He felt Victor's letter in his pocket, pulled it out, and began to read.

My Dear Sasha,

You have a great vision and courage to pursue it. Get comfortable being uncomfortable and never give up.

Your description of your workplace gave me the chills. This is one of the biggest issues with a democracy and with capitalism: education. As Thomas Jefferson said, "An educated citizenry is a vital requisite for our survival as a free people." The workers at Water Macro came from a repressive economic culture. If they could now experience a kinder, fairer, lighter touch from management that respected them as unique individuals, they would respond very positively. This new culture could be like being around a blended family of individuals who grew up in malfunctioning families of origin. They could work smoothly together. Pastor Eric Huffman refers to this experience as "the family that works." The people running Water Macro appear to be simply ignorant of how to create a work culture that responds to the marketplace in a way that increases profits and creates a culture of respect. I'm literally shaking my head in disbelief. Nevertheless, the last thing anyone should want to do is to bring in more government to make people act a certain way. People do have the ability to be vicious, greedy and controlling. They can also be creative, compassionate and accepting of different approaches. This is actually a perfect opportunity for you to exercise your leadership skills and help to create a different culture at Water Macro.

You are so busy right now, you probably have not noticed the articles recently published about President Obama's manipulation of the press in order to push through his agenda for Iran. In this case, he used Ben Rhodes, a national security advisor, who knows how to push information out using the tools of the Internet and relatively inexperienced young White House reporters. The point is, the President created the foreign policy he wanted to create, i.e., arming Iran with nuclear weapons by sidestepping some of his advisors and manipulating the press. It's fairly crafty, completely cynical and utterly frightening. I can't tell you how familiar this sort of dishonest behavior is to someone from a Communist country. There, control of the press and the truth is vital to controlling the people's liberties.

As you enter into the swamp of business ethics and government ethics, you will soon see that the struggle to be, as Confucius says, "a gentleman," meaning a person of high moral behavior, is a struggle that is common for us all. What is infuriating is that each person's struggle affects the struggle of their neighbor, creating so many waves that it is hard to swim, hard to even stay alive.

Your employers have done what, in my opinion, Obama did: they have capitalized on a human weakness—believing without questioning— and used it to profit themselves, recreating, as you said, "a gulag mentality." Did they manipulate these people as knowingly as Obama manipulated inexperienced reporters with Tweets about a "moderate" Iran? I cannot say. I can only say that as you move through the swamp, your only weapon is your own moral code. Follow it and others will follow you.

A key ingredient in solving problems without creating new laws and policies is frequent, extensive communication. Asking, listening, experimenting and investigating failures and successes—all within the framework of team conversations. What is ironic is that many people who champion less government interference in business actually cling to outdated, top-down organizational structures in their businesses. They want Big Brother to let go, but they can't stop controlling everyone and everything. Of course they lose money that way.

You say that most of the employees are afraid to speak up. OK, you speak up. Set up a meeting with the owners and lay out for them the reality they cannot see, i.e., that their employees hate their jobs, they are less efficient because they work too much, have no say and feel dominated.

Bring in information that they can read that shows that the more contribution and ownership people feel toward their jobs, the more money the company makes.

Finally, introduce the idea of competing in a global marketplace. Show them that they are losing market share to other filtration companies located all over the world. They need to find an edge because it's not just about making a better product, it's about finding a better way to support the customer. For example, Water Macro probably offers just about the same products and services as any number of companies in that Standard Industrial Classification code. To gain an edge, turn to the employees— all of them—and find out from their experiences where a customer's need exists. Maybe the delivery people have noticed that one customer needs better logistically planned deliveries. Maybe the computer tech has noticed that there are long wait times for certain pages on the website. Perhaps a salesperson has noticed that some customers are asking for in-depth chemical tests of the water. Maybe some customers have one need and other customers have another need. These needs may not have anything to do directly with water, but by meeting these needs, Water Macro can create a value add to their business—and additional revenue. What is the secret weapon? It's the employees—all of them. Human beings are always a company's greatest asset. There is a good book about this, *The Squaredime Letters*, by C.J. Coolidge. I learned all of these ideas from reading that book and others like it. They're not my ideas; I just did the research.

To implement these changes, the Water Macro people will need to let go of micro-managing their employees and engage them in brainstorming exercises so that they can start flexing their voices and ideas. After awhile, the owners may find that people from the United States bring more initiative to the job. I don't know, actually. Let's wait and see. The former "Communists" may bloom just as I did and as you are.

A great book about bringing brainstorming into the workplace and using it as a tool to increase market share is *Power Brainstorming*, by Hazel Wagner. There are many great tools and ideas that someone can use to get out of the box and push through economic walls. You can find them in the bookstore or the library, through Google or by asking people what they did. You get what you ask for, so ask. Forget about scarcity mentality, you're creating abundance.

Many, many studies have been completed about workplace culture and how it can increase profits. The cutting-edge information we have says that a flat workplace where the "boss" acts as a guide rather than as an authority is the way to go. Here is the link to a review of the book *Reinventing Organizations*, by Frédéric Laloux: jarche.com/2014/05/reinventing-organizations-review/. This book gives you a bigger picture as to how a self-managing structure works. He summarizes it saying, ". . . the key role of a CEO is in holding the space so that teams can self-manage. It means keeping others, like investors, from screwing things up."

I can tell you that in my own office, I employ a small staff. I'm a financial advisor, so it's a little bit different from being a manufacturer, in that my product and my intellectual expertise are the same. In my office, we have weekly staff meetings, which are open-ended. During these, I encourage everyone to discuss operations, to make suggestions and to bounce new ideas off of one another. I keep talking and keep them talking. When one of my staff *identifies a personal goal, I support them in realizing that goal. Sometimes that means investing money in education, sometimes it means flexing work hours or duties. It always means that I listen. I ask myself, "What can I learn from this person?" Even in the act of listening and then repeating back to an individual the problems or issues they mentioned, I am communicating respect and support of them as employees and as individuals.*

I'm reminded, as I say this, of China's recent behavior. You might have read about the way that the Chinese government is propping up many manufacturing businesses so that the global market is glutted with materials like aluminum and steel—so much so that many people in the United States have had to shut down operations. Such interference by the government, refusing to allow plants to fail and shut down, has had devastating effects around the world.

That being said, Sasha, the mature, kind and common-sense approach to failure is to stop doing what you have been doing and to do something else. In terms of employees, there is nothing wrong with ending an employment relationship if it is not working for either party. There is nothing wrong with shutting down a business if it is not profitable over time. In fact, this is good and healthy. Let yourself accept that you may need to let go of this job or they may need to let go of you. Do this mentally and emotionally before you begin to have a conversation with them. They will feel your detachment and it will help them truly hear what you have to say.

I am what is called a "Stephen minister" in my church. To be a Stephen minister, I took classes in how to listen and how to be of real service to someone. I'm grateful for the training because it has informed me in all aspects of my life. I've learned through trial and error to hold my employees with an open hand and to listen from a place of curiosity.

Stephen was a follower of Jesus Christ and a leader. Soon after Jesus was crucified, the early Christians formed a communal group in Jerusalem where they shared all that they had with one another freely. They also gave succor to the sick, the poor and those who were grieving and alone. The other people in the town began to be afraid of this new group. Their actions of generosity and love toward strangers in need were so different from anything they had ever seen before. They felt accused in their own hearts to see such kindness demonstrated to people whom they had long ignored. You can probably guess what happened next: Violence erupted. The townspeople turned on Stephen one day and they stoned him to death, making him the first Christian martyr.

We who lived under the oppression of a Communist government can clearly see the difference between the early communal sharing of the Christians and the horror we endured. The difference is that the first one came from the heart and was not compelled by law or fear. The practice of true moral values such as loving one's neighbor as one's self is radically different from the material power structure of our societies today and those thousands of years ago. So different that one can barely tolerate the other.

Today, perhaps we can employ incremental change. We can gradually move toward compassionate choices in the workplace and in the economy. It's going to take careful research to prove that change works, and it's going to take many thoughtful, curious and respectful conversations.

I'm looking forward to hearing how your conversations with the management and staff at Water Macro go. I think you can use this experience both in running your own company and also when you begin to host grassroots conversations about free-market solutions. Someday, this experience may be part of a book or article or speech. This is the life of a leader in a free country, Sasha. You will make a great role model for many other new American citizens.

There are capitalist mentors all around us if we look carefully. For example, the former governor of Indiana, Mitch Daniels, simply applied appropriate budget cuts and efficient use of government funds. Without raising taxes, he saved money and jobs. You can find out more about him in his book, Keeping the Republic: Saving America by Trusting American Voters. Hey, I know I've mentioned a lot of books in this letter. The questions never stop and neither does the research.

I'm looking forward to reading your poems. Please send me your book at the address below. I suppose we can start using traditional mailing methods if you would like. I do trust you, Sasha, but you're right, I need to trust you more. I too am looking forward to a time when we can meet face-to-face.

You seem to have a gift for forming strong friendships. Crandall sounds like someone who values you as a friend and is interested in you. It's a rare person who both listens and understands. Suki and you must have a lot of fun together; having fun matters a lot when you're working hard and thinking hard. It's just as important as anything else. That's one of the things I liked the most about your mother: She and I could have fun just sitting at a stake-out or cleaning our weapons. Once, we shared a wiretap for three days. Welcome to your old-fashioned spy parents' memories.

Sasha, I know your early years were spent in a rather remote region of the world and that you come from a Muslim tribe and were raised by a yogi mother. These days of ISIS and war make it harder and harder for people to separate the religion of Islam from those terrorists who have appropriated the word "Islamic" and some other catchphrases of the religion. We must make the effort, however. Otherwise, we will become like the extremists we so despise. Thank you for being open to hearing about my spiritual journey as a Christian. I hope I can be as welcoming should you ever wish to talk about yours.

Here is a picture of me a few years before you were born. My hair is white now, my waist a little thicker and I no longer climb mountains. Life is a wonderful struggle, Sasha: full of tension, conversations, change and friendship. Someday you and I will sit down to a cup of tea before a roaring fire. Until then, I remain,
Affectionately yours,
Victor

Chapter 6

Your Ideas Are Valuable

A popular government without popular information or the means of acquiring it, is but a prologue to a farce, or a tragedy, or perhaps both.

— James Madison

"Here it is." Sasha walked into his newly outfitted lab in the downstairs kitchen.

Suki walked around, taking note of all of his improvements and the well-stocked supplies in the cabinets.

"Beautiful. Beautiful," she said and then shot him a smile. He'd begun to think of her smiles as fiery arrows—they always seemed to break through a fog he didn't even know he had. Suki knew about labs, having been on the medical track for a few years. She looked around and up at the air ducts in the ceiling. "You might want to put in a filter here." He nodded gratefully and made a note.

Just then, his phone rang. It was Julia. "Excuse me, Suki."

"Hey, Julia! How are you?"

"Hi, Sasha. I'm doing well. I hadn't heard from you and thought I would check in. How's everything going for you in San Francisco?"

"It's going really well, Julia. I'm actually just down here in a spare kitchen in the house where I live that I've converted into a lab."

"Wow! Send me a picture," she said.

"Will do. Hey, my friend Suki is down here with me. I wish you guys could meet. She's so great."

"Oh, so glad to hear you're making new friends, Sasha." Julia's voice was more cheerful and happy than he had ever heard it. He remembered her as a very serious person. "Please call me back when you have more time, Sasha. I want to hear more about how it's going for you there."

"OK. OK. Sounds good. I'll call you maybe tomorrow around five. Is that OK? I'm usually on the bus or train about then."

"Yes." They said goodbye, and Sasha looked up to see Suki testing his gas line for air.

"So . . .," she said, looking at him with an unusual expression that he could not translate.

"That was Julia," Sasha said, and Suki nodded absently, investigating his lighting.

"Is she your . . . ?"

"Ah, no . . . umm, no. She's not my girlfriend, if that's what you're asking. No. She's a friend. She's helped me out a little bit since I had the accident water skiing."

"Oh," Suki said. "So, she's the girl you met to go water skiing with when you hit your head?"

Sasha nodded. A realization was dawning on him. He could almost hear his mother's voice as she chopped the chicken: "Truth . . . tell the whole truth. Don't wait for someone to ask you—that is a form of lying."

"The truth is, Suki, that Julia did want to be my girlfriend, I guess, but I told her I wasn't interested in dating anyone since I've been through so much change in my family."

Suki nodded. "Do you still feel that way?"

Sasha looked at Suki, and he felt a crystalline leaf fall from an unknown tree into his heart. What was that? Sasha, in all of his life, had never felt heart to heart communication. It was apart from his mind, it was alive. His heart was actually talking and living an emotional life apart from his brain. He cleared his throat and slowly eased onto a barstool.

"Logically, my mind says, 'Yes, absolutely.' I just . . . The truth is, Suki, I've never actually dated anyone. I've never had a girlfriend. I had a mother and father, and I lost them. It just seems like I can't go beyond that fact. When Julia . . . when I was with Julia, I really liked her. She's kindhearted and . . . ."

"And?" Suki's green eyes were shooting arrows at him again. "Beautiful?"

He nodded. "Yes, she's pretty." He gazed at his friend as she stood near the cooling unit. "She's pretty, but . . . . Let me ask you something, Suki. If you were interested in dating someone, would I be in the running? Would you ever consider me?"

Suki smiled, and he could tell that she was relieved to have the tables turned away from his choices to her own. She nodded. "Yes. I would. I like you. I'd like to date you, and if you're not available, then I'm good with our friendship, Sasha." She sighed and laughed. "I've had a couple of boyfriends. It's really best to be good friends, and if romance happens, well, hold it with a loose hand."

Sasha nodded, jotting down her advice mentally. "Good to know. I know nothing about the subject. I'm flattered, Suki. You...you are like a warm fire on a dark night. When I'm with you, I feel great. . . ."

"But?" she said.

"But, I can't go past a friendship. I just can't with you or with anyone. My heart has some sort of . . . ." He touched his heart, " . . . some sort of . . . ."

"What?"

"I don't know." He sighed, "It hurts. I feel . . . like it is . . . ." He felt tears suddenly welling up, and he looked away because he knew that he wanted to say, "Crying."

Suki came over to him and spoke very softly, "It's OK. It's OK, Sasha." She pointed out the patio door and said, "Look."

He saw in the upwardly sloping hillside a deer—no, gradually he saw standing among the trees, six deer: six adolescents stood together, eating fruit fallen from the loquat trees. He took Suki's hand in his own and squeezed it.

"They've left home without their mother for the first time."

"At least they're not alone."

They quietly retreated upstairs, and Suki said goodbye at the door, waving. She was untroubled, he could see, by their conversation. He shook his head: two women. How did this happen? He wanted so badly to turn to Yusup and tell him; he had always brought all of his life problems to his father until he went to London. He shook his head again: two fathers. How did this happen? He smiled then and went back down to watch the deer alone.

The next day at work, Sasha knocked on Marlena's office door. "Come in," she called immediately. So few employees came to see her, she registered shock on her face when Sasha stepped inside. She motioned to the chair in front of her desk. "How can I help you, Sasha?"

Sasha did not sit down. "Hey. I would like to set up a time, a meeting, with you and Jan. Would that be possible?"

"What about?"

"Marlena, I've noticed that there are some ways that Water Macro could possibly increase profits. I've researched it, and I just wanted to sit down with the two of you and discuss my ideas."

Marlena blinked. "Oh. Well. Why don't you just send us an email?"

Sasha smiled and nodded. "I thought of that, Marlena, but some of the ideas really need me to explain them. Also, I'd just like to communicate with you both in person." He felt that he had pushed through her initial resistance and he pressed his advantage, saying, "I've got my research written down, and I can bring it to the meeting. This has to do with the filtered-water market and is very specific to Water Macro."

Marlena was clearly swimming in new waters. An hourly employee acting in the capacity of an operations/marketing manager. Hmm. She shrugged. Why not? "Sure. OK. It looks like Jan and I are both free on Thursday at about eight AM."

"I will see you both on Thursday at eight AM, then." Sasha stuck out his hand, and she tentatively shook it and nodded.

He left Marlena's office and returned to his station in the workroom, putting on his lab coat as he went. The other workers watched him intently, having seen him in her office through the glass dividing walls. They sensed danger. Later, at lunch, Daniel approached him, asking, "How's it going?" Sasha had anticipated this. He wanted to tenderize the other employees, preparing their minds for the possibility of change. He wanted them all to start talking to one another openly and without fear."

"Daniel. Hi. It's going great." He pulled out his list of inefficient processes and operations and showed it to Daniel. "I made this list of possible improvements. I'm going to talk to Marlena and Jan about it on Thursday."

Daniel nodded imperceptibly. He kept his eyes averted. He did not reach out to take the list to read it. Sasha continued casually and cheerfully, "I was hoping some of you guys might help me with it, you know, review it and make any changes you think are best."

The room was still noisy, but Sasha could tell that other employees nearby were listening. Sasha, without thinking, seized the moment. He began to talk loudly as if he were on stage.

He took the list and walked over to a large, round table where 10 people were sitting. "Please pass it around to each table," he said. Please write your changes or new ideas, and give it to the next person." Sasha laid the paper on the table with authority and bowed slightly to the room. "Your ideas are important. You are valuable."

He quietly left the lunchroom and walked out onto the small, concrete courtyard where people went to smoke. He kept his back to the sliding glass doors, just looking up into the sky. He waited there for 20 minutes, until lunch was almost over. Then he slid the door open and went inside. The room was empty—early—and the list of recommended improvements lay on the last table. He picked it up. It was full. Every square inch on the front and the back was covered in broken English sentences describing filtration and delivery problems. He did not find anywhere on the paper, however, a single mention of the workers' own needs as employees.

Sasha recalled hearing on the news that President Obama was issuing an executive order that would allow employees to receive overtime pay, even if they were exempt. He made a note to mention this to Victor in his next letter. This was a classic example of a longstanding abusive practice by employers—not paying employees for working overtime—that was ignored by conservative leaders until government responded to an outcry with more legislation.

Later, Sasha prepared his statistics and research regarding company profit margins within the water market. He found evidence of open, flat systems of operation being stronger and more flexible when confronted with a changing client profile.

When Thursday came, Sasha buttoned up his shirt and put on his tie. He turned left instead of right when he came in the door at Water Macro. Marlena and Jan were waiting for him in Marlena's office. They were both wearing curious expressions. Just seeing them sitting in the office expectantly waiting for him, Sasha could see that they had no idea how their business model affected the lives of their employees. They had started something and it had seemed to work well, and, although they made changes now and then, they really had never questioned the idea of using a mechanical factory business model. Or had they? Would they be open to real change? Were they flexible, or were they insecure tyrants? All these questions and more ran through Sasha's mind as he sat down on the edge of his chair. Without ado, he handed them each a presentation folder and then, with a few words of explanation, began to run the slideshow he had created on his laptop.

They carefully watched the slideshow and referred to the information in their packets. At pause points, they asked questions. Jan asked, "So, if all of the employees are being equally tapped during brainstorming sessions for ideas to solve business problems, does this mean that their salaries become more equalized, that everyone would make the same amount?"

Sasha responded, "Not at first. As profits increase and the workforce becomes more adept at spotting weaknesses and responding to them, then, yes, salaries would increase and equalize."

Later, Marlena referred to the issues in production and distribution that the employees had identified: "So, have the employees also offered solutions to these problems?"

Sasha responded, "No. They have not been asked to provide solutions at this point. To do that would be to change the structure and the culture of the organization. That is something that requires your . . . ," he hesitated to use the word *permission*. Finally, he said, ". . . guidance."

Marlena then pointed to the list of employee issues that Sasha had created on his own. Among them were issues relating to taking breaks, work hours, flexibility of work hours, part-time and job-sharing availability to fit into employee goals, and the lack of onsite childcare, a big issue with many of the employees.

"You're basically saying that the employees are miserable here and only work here because they're used to being repressed in Communist countries. That they see this company as a kind of police state . . . I mean . . . in their minds? It's not a police state," she added defensively.

Sasha nodded and shook his head quizzically. "It's a bit of a puzzle. I thought you purposefully hired these people for this reason. At least at first, I thought that was your plan, which is pretty cynical. Then later, I began to see that perhaps you just noticed that a certain type of person had a great work ethic and you didn't necessarily hire them for being easy to control."

The two women, instead of reacting to this veiled accusation, ignored it. They sat quietly rereading the list of issues. They were engrossed in carefully scanning the charts Sasha had presented to them regarding profitability in their industry globally and nationally. They didn't seem to be bothered or insulted; he studied their body language. At the same time, they did not make any reply to his statement. Time passed. The clock ticked. The two women sat reading and reading the information before them.

"So," Jan finally spoke. "What you're saying is that . . . what you're suggesting to us is that we *literally change* almost *every single thing* except for a handful of practices and procedures. Is that correct?"

Before Sasha could answer, she continued, "You're suggesting that we flatten hierarchies, start brainstorming as a function of operations that includes all employees, alter our filtration processes, distribution processes, and customer relations. Also, that we be willing to do this *continually* to respond to market needs, even on an individual basis, so we could be running multiple campaigns simultaneously?"

"And," Marlena jumped in, "you're suggesting that we delegate our employees as their own managers and let them conform their jobs more around their lifestyle desires, sort of like you suggest that we conform the product and services we offer around our customers' desires . . . very customized?"

Sasha gulped and nodded. "You've got it. You've really got it." He sighed. "I know it's a lot of change and will continue to be a lot of change. At the same time, it opens Water Macro up to expansion in ways it is not open today."

Jan leaned back in her chair and flexed every muscle in her body. Sasha's eyes widened. Wow. She was like a golden lion, he thought, stretching on the plain before a kill. "Is she going to kill me?" he wondered.

"I like it," Jan said looking at Marlena with a big grin and cracking her knuckles.

Marlena kept turning the pages back and forth. "These charts are interesting, Sasha. I will have to drill down to the stats and do some more reading. I will also have to create a financial plan around this and run it by some other people."

"You mean, you're going to consider becoming a 'Teal,' or flat, organization that runs on its employees' creative power?" Sasha couldn't believe his ears. He had recently read the books *Reinventing Organizations*, by Frédéric Laloux, and *Team of Teams*, by Gen. Stanley McChrystal, but had not yet met anyone who was willing to implement their nonhierarchical concepts.

Marlena laughed. "What? Did you think we were with the People's Republic or something?" she joked, but he could feel a little bite in it. "No, Sasha. We acknowledge that the structure we've had in place is not the best. Frankly, we've been searching for new ideas for quite a while. We found some of this that you brought in, but it wasn't put together in such a way that we could see it fitting into a whole. For instance, we were looking at marketing models that conformed more to specialized customer desires."

"Right," Jan interjected. "But we couldn't see how to alter the workforce to make that a reality. The stuff we were reading was staying with a hierarchical model that required creating a bigger staff of marketers and customer service people. We were not willing to do that right away. This makes a lot more sense because everyone who works here already has an intimate knowledge of the product and the customer base. We just need to encourage them to share it—via brainstorming sessions."

"The only problem I see," Sasha said, "is that you have a frightened, repressed workforce that isn't using their imaginations. It may not be possible to get them to change their ways. I hate to say it, but they may be too shut down mentally and emotionally to do this."

"Let's start out slow, maybe," Jan offered. "Perhaps we can set up a cafeteria for them and get their suggestions regarding that and see how it goes."

Marlena and Sasha nodded.

The meeting ended with Jan and Marlena promising to sit down with Sasha again in the next 30 days.

"OK," Sasha said, mentally marking the time. "I will need to have a prototype in hand by then. If the employees are really serious about making these changes, I may be able to pitch a partnership to them."

He put on his lab coat and walked into the work area. Everyone was busy. He put on his gloves and ignited his burner. He couldn't wait until later that evening when he could write to Victor. Amazing news; it could have gone in a completely different direction. Was this *luck*? He heard his mother's voice telling him, as she had told him every day of his life with her, "You do not attract what you want in life, Sasha. You attract what you *are*. Be good." He smiled into the blue flame.

That afternoon, around 5 PM, on the train, Sasha took out his pen and began to write to Victor. Then, he let the pen drop and, with one movement, picked up his phone and dialed Yusup's phone number. Yusup had a landline, not a cell phone. He'd often pointed out that a landline phone was a superior part of the past he was not going to lose. It would be 7 PM in Austin, Sasha thought. Just as the phone started to ring, he hung up. No. No. Why open a can of worms?

He returned to his letter. Just then, his phone rang, showing Yusup's number. He answered it nervously, "Hello?" On the other end, he heard a series of clicks and rustling noises, then the unmistakable sound of a baby babbling into the receiver. Ah, Sasha smiled and thought, "My little brother." Sasha listened to the baby happily until the receiver somehow found its way back into the cradle. "Maybe this was better," he thought, and settled down to write, feeling almost giddy. He realized this was his first real connection to the father he'd lost since he flew to London over a year ago. Not only was it a connection, it was good to meet his "replacement" up front and to extend to him good will. It was a very good start in what he now realized he wanted—a new and different family, but definitely a family.

Dear Victor,

I hope this conventionally mailed letter finds you well. I hope that as you pulled it from your mailbox, you had a feeling of being firmly in the private sector and out of the business of spying once and for all.

I'm writing to tell you some good news. I did speak up as you advised to the co-owners of Water Macro. They were shockingly receptive. I still have a hard time believing how open they were/are to the reorganization ideas I presented to them. They did say that they had been researching and questioning their practices for some time before I showed up. It is an amazing synchronicity, don't you think? It made me think of something Nur used to say to me: "You don't attract what you want, you attract what you are. Be good." Did she ever say this to you?

I'm thinking now that I might be able to come up with a first rendition of a prototype to present to them in the next 30 days. Who knows? They might turn out to be good partners. It would be really the only avenue by which I could launch a small business. Even with the savings I'm able to put away, there's no way I can pay the various fees and taxes required anytime soon.

I suspect that as they make changes, they will rely on me, and my role in the company will change. This will be a good experience for me as I prepare to run my own company. I also suspect that I will have a say in new people they hire. They're going to need to bring on some new people and use them as role models—seeds—sort of to change the culture. I really had no idea how closely a company's culture conforms to the mindset of those who set it up. It would be nice to see individuals at work just be themselves instead of narcissistic reflections of founders and bosses. LOL. I remember asking my neighbor how she got a job at a large call center that sells business information. She said that she wore a pretty dress to the job interview and that she had the same first name as the manager's wife. Not a professional picture of American business, I'm afraid. There really has to be a more scientific way of selecting personnel than the whims and misguided power plays of most managers.

By the way, I noticed a new law going into effect that would pay salaried workers who make up to 48K overtime wages. Doesn't this look just like the kind of reform that needed to be applied using a free-market system instead of a government intervention? Isn't this just the sort of problem relating to poverty that conservatives could have solved before now?

I'm writing you on the train home from work, and I'm almost at my stop. I will drop this in the box on the corner. It is a relief to me to rely on postal carriers. I guess I'm not James Bond material.
Warm wishes,
Sasha

Early the next morning, at 4 AM, Sasha's phone rang again. Again, he saw Yusup's number on the screen. "Hello?" he answered sleepily, wondering if the baby was up so early.

"Sasha?" Yusup's voice startled him awake.

"Chichi." A silence hung between them. Neither man spoke. Finally, Yusup ventured, "Sasha, I'm so happy to hear from you. I was so worried. I'm sorry. I'm sorry I have not been a good father. You are always my son. Please don't go away."

"Chichi," Sasha said again, his heart swelling with happiness. "I have missed you. How are you?"

Yusup laughed a kind of laugh that sounded like weeping and laughing at the same time. "I am well. We are well. I have another son now."

"I know. I met him."

"You met him?"

"Yes, he must have pushed the callback button on the phone yesterday. I answered, and a baby talked to me for at least five minutes. He sounds like he is full of mischief."

"Yes, yes," Yusup said and blew his nose. "You must come and meet him. Come see us. Where are you?"

"I'm in San Francisco. I'm starting a new business. It's about water."

"Oh." Sasha could almost hear Yusup processing this information. Then he switched from Mandarin to English to gleefully exclaim, "You American! You capitalist!"

"Yes, I'm an American, Chichi," Sasha said, laughing. He felt more relaxed now, and he wondered if he should ask his father about Nur, but decided against it. There was one matter, though, about which he needed Yusup's advice. He paused and cleared his throat. "Umm, guess what?"

"What?" Yusup guessed. "You have a girlfriend?"

"No. No, but I have two friends who are women. . . ."

"You must choose." His father stated this flatly.

"Do I have to?"

"No. You can just stay friends with both. But, someday you will have to choose or find a third woman."

"That could be a long time from now."

"Yes. No rush. Man can be old like me and still have young wife . . . like me." Yusup's voice carried in it an edge of exhaustion and resignation.

Sasha did not feel satisfied.

"I . . . well . . .," he stammered, sighing heavily and then bursting out in frustration, "But . . . I don't *want* to be old. What would help me choose, Chichi? How do I choose?"

"Man is happy when wife is happy," Yusup spoke slowly as if realizing this for the first time. "I did not know this before, but I do now. You must choose the woman whom you can make happy the best."

Sasha let this sink in. It seemed logical. At the same time, what lay beneath the waves of "happiness"? It was a murky sea. He bowed his head, put on his respectful voice, and said, "OK. Good advice. Thank you, Chichi."

"You call me every week? This a good time?" Sasha nodded into the phone, relief flooding his body, and said, "Yes. Yes. Yes."

They said their goodbyes just as Al was flinging his legs off the side of the bed. Sasha ran to catch him, his heart singing.

Since he had just mailed his letter to Victor, Sasha did not check the mailbox that morning. He did begin checking it two days later, but no reply. He was just walking out of the house on Friday morning, a week after the meeting with Marlena and Jan, to catch the bus down the hill, when a fat, gray pigeon perched on the porch railing caught his attention. It had around one leg a tiny leather holster containing a plastic capsule. The bird let Sasha unsnap the holster and remove the capsule. Inside, he found what he intuitively knew was Victor's reply on a thin piece of paper. He replaced the empty capsule, and the bird flew away. Sasha watched it circle once, then head north. Huh. "I guess some people are a little more James Bond than others," he muttered as he put the letter into his jacket and struck off at a fast pace to catch the bus. He might have to run all the way down the hill if he missed it. He could do it, but he'd rather ride. He did catch the bus and the train after that. He was able to scan through Victor's letter. Later that day, he read it again very slowly.

Dear Sasha,

What great news! I am celebrating with you! It was your careful research that carried the day, wasn't it? Any enterprise, great or small, begins and ends with research.

Even the most important job of being a citizen requires that we know how the government works and what the issues are. Why do you think that so few United States citizens actually do the work required to be citizens? Why do you think they fixate on Presidential elections and fail to vote for congressional candidates? Why do they complain but never read? What are your thoughts on this?

Politics, politics, huh? I know you are wondering why I sent my letter by homing pigeon instead of by the U.S. Post Office. I was actually stationed in the Russian Navy for five years and had many enjoyable hours of training and raising homing pigeons on an aircraft carrier. It is still a part of the culture in the Middle East. I sent Ralph the Pigeon with your letter because I get a kick out of it. Believe me, I'm not trying to avoid postal carriers, I just have a few homing pigeons and couldn't resist.

As for the medical report attached: Sasha, I am grateful for your trust and openness toward me as your father. Still, just to calm any questions that might arise regarding my paternity, I have sent you my DNA test results. You can run your own test and have a technician compare the results. That way, when I irritate you or worse and you are inclined to declare us unrelated, you can know that we are joined both by affection and by biology.

I actually met you once before. You may not remember. I drove you and Nur out of China, over the mountains and into Turkey. I carried you up the stairs to the hotel room in Ankara. You were only a little boy. I've cherished that memory many times over the years. It was the last time I held your mother in my arms. And, yes, she did say that phrase about "attracting what you are" to me as well. The old yogi who raised her did a remarkable job, I must say. I look at the blank faces of some young people today, and I wonder what creative and brilliant minds lie asleep under an addiction of AV stimulation. Am I being age-ist? Have I stereotyped all young people, ascribing emptiness to their stoicism?

I do wonder who values being good or, as Socrates described it, having "virtue"? Two of the candidates who are running for office, Trump and Clinton, both have ethical shortcomings. In a society where people are invested in research and in civic action, would they have emerged as candidates in the general election? I doubt it. These two people are a reflection of a society that is too distracted to pay close attention.

Some would say we U.S. citizens are hard-pressed to survive and must work to pay taxes and high prices—so much so that we do not have the time to really participate in our own government, leaving it to the lobbyists to divide it up among themselves.

Others would say that the wealthy buy government instead of participating in it as the Founding Fathers intended. If James Madison or Thomas Jefferson were here now, it would be like you or I looking out over the redwood forest, blackened by fire and strewn with tattered American flags. I'm sure they would gasp at the state of our Republic.

Nevertheless, I am a bit pleased to see Donald Trump turning Washington insiders upside down. Why not? He is shaking up the Republican Party—a party that has lost its attraction for the American people. It needs to be tossed and smashed like outdated teacups, and why not by a bull like Trump? It's interesting to watch what's left of the democratic process in action.

Don't let me discourage you, Sasha. Sometimes, my mind becomes discouraged when I read the news. Then, I look at your bright future and realize that there are millions more like you: thinking, caring entrepreneurs and human beings. You are our hope. I encourage you to schedule the time each month to participate in your state and local government as well as to inform yourself about national issues. Be what you want to see, then you will attract what you are.

Regarding your question about conservatives coming up with a solution to people working overtime and not getting paid for it: Didn't I already tell you the solution to that problem? Regardless of your education, insist on either being a contractor or being a nonexempt employee. This is the free-market solution to that problem. People just need to know it and do it. It's a matter of education rather than legislation. Eventually, businesses would have to conform to the employee demand for fair pay.

You mention that you may possibly step into the role of HR advisor or even act as a hiring manager at Water Macro. Certainly, that is a possibility. I agree that it would be great experience for you as you prepare to launch your own company.

Along with my DNA chart, I also included a chart I use in conducting business. It is called Passion, Action, Results, or PAR for short. This is a kind of questionnaire that I use when interviewing people for four distinct types of positions: Revenue Finder, Relationship Builder, Closer and Processor. You might find it useful. When you select employees, you are really a relationship manager. You're considering first the employee and their family at the center of the circle you call your business. Then, in the next concentric circle, you have your vendors and suppliers. In the next circle are your clients. Finally, the last circle is the world at large. Many business owners start with their clients and the world at large and do not take the relationships with their employees and their vendors seriously. Your employees and your vendors make up the core of your operations, so take them very seriously. That being said, here are the four types of employees I mentioned:

- *Revenue Finder—This is a person who is hospitable, gregarious and likes to socialize. They are constantly exchanging and refining information, always connecting, communicating and moving forward.*
- *Relationship Builder—This person sees the big picture when it comes to relationships. They are laid back, comfortable with themselves, and accommodating. These are not abrasive people. These are people who know how to meld into a community and strengthen it by their willingness to compromise and contribute.*
- *Closer—This is a person who always has the bottom line in mind. They see the facts. They're able to listen to objections, put pen to paper, and show solutions to those objections.*
- *Processor—This is a person who has no problem conforming to rules. They are the scientists and auditors and legal people who grind out the spreadsheets, contracts, permits, licenses, letters, guidelines and checks. This can be one or multiple people.*

We're assuming that you are a business owner. Before you start interviewing people, you need to figure out how you allot your own energy. When you figure this out, then you know what kind of people you are looking to hire.

I.   *How much of your expenses were you able to charge off to your business?*

II. *How much do you pay yourself? What is the economic value of your time? For example, if someone else were to do the processing that you now do, would it be worth it to the business to sustain both the salary and the benefits of that person ($\approx \$30,000$)?*

III. *How much is it costing the business to pay you to do work you can delegate? If you are doing work that drains you and you are not happy doing it, then you're not using your own strengths or the strengths of your employees or potential employees effectively.*

Now, that you know the context of your own financial situation, ask yourself the questions 1-7. When you find out what it is that you need someone else to do while you focus 95% of your time on your passion, you are ready to start interviewing other people.

1. *How much time do you spend on the following? Please place a number representing a percentage of your time:*
   - *New business _____*
   - *Relationships _____*
   - *Closing _____*
   - *Paperwork _____*
2. *Which of these would you do, if you could, 95% of the time?*
3. *When you know the answer to question 2 above, then ask yourself or the person you want to delegate responsibilities to if you/they can find a way to commit 75% more of their time to what they feel most drawn to, or their passion?*
4. *What drains you? (Sometimes people spend 50% of their time on what they hate.)*
5. *Rank the other two roles at 2% or 3%.*
6. *What actions do you have to take to change your energy allotments?*
7. *What do you most enjoy doing outside of work?*

As a business owner, you now know more about yourself. You know what you enjoy and what drains you.

- *What would you accomplish in the first 90 days if you could commit 95% of your time to your passion?*
- *How many hours do you need to be freed up to make X dollars per week?*
- *What would happen if you could release 15 hours per week? Where would your time go? This is the bottom line.*
- *Now, you know that you need to hire someone to take care of your question 4 activity, the one that drains you the most.*

Sasha, I know you may have already crunched this sort of thing in college business courses. Nevertheless, I wanted to share this with you because I use it all the time, and PAR has been an invaluable tool for me.

When you find out what you want, then you can plan for your future. For example, I have a friend who runs a business. He never really sat down and examined the kind of work he enjoys doing versus the kind of work that he does. He would like to retire, but he has to keep working another three years in order to afford the kind of retirement he wants to have. In particular, he wants to spend a large sum on his daughter's wedding. She is the apple of his eye. All of these things are things that he wants. Our desires drive us far more than our needs.

Take your own desires into account when you are creating your personal profit and loss statement. Everyone needs to have a living profit and loss statement that goes through life with them.

I advise my clients to put aside a certain amount of money for each of their children and then, when the child reaches college age, to explain to them, "Here is X amount of money. You can spend it or you can pay for college. Regardless of what you do, live within your means."

In today's world in the United States, many people spend more money than they actually take in. In fact, studies show that debt payment has replaced saving in American households.

This is how the government behaves as well. I was just reading about the bullet train commissioned by the Obama Administration for the state of California. Billions of dollars have been spent to set up this form of transport, but the train is nonexistent. Instead of recognizing that they wasted money and made a mistake, the government is spending even more money on this black hole.

As we've discussed before, governments stop existing solely to perform their limited functions very soon after they come into being. Literally within months, they transform into power rather than service entities, and their goal becomes to support their own existence rather than act as a subsidiary to the people's will and rights.

When Edward Snowden blew the whistle on the over-surveillance of the U.S. government on its people, he was the second man to come forward. The first man who brought the same NSA issues to the fore 10 years ago, Tom Drake, was fired, stripped of his pension, wrongly accused and now works as a clerk in an Apple store. He followed the rules and he was crushed.

When the senior official in the Department of Defense, John Crane, in charge of protecting whistleblowers under the law, spoke up for Drake, he too lost his job and was ruined. This was a good guy inside the system standing up for the law and he was illegally destroyed by the people with whom he worked. Snowden saw that. He knew that going through the system is suicide.

We rely on whistleblowers. We need to protect ourselves from government abuses by those from within who are true civil servants. Why on earth would Obama decry Snowden, saying that he should follow the proper channels for reporting abuses when he was fully aware of how both Drake and Crane were destroyed?

Sure, Obama has supported whistleblowers who report corporations who are defrauding the federal government. He's terrible regarding national security and great regarding corporate fraud. Why? I'm sure we could find the answer if we understood his understanding of his own personal power. Why would I say such a thing? I say it because it is the nature of human beings who hold vast control over the lives of others.

Another example that few people are aware of is a recent net neutrality regulation that the Obama Administration forced onto the burgeoning television industry. Described as "anti-business," the new FCC regulations effectively hobble TV just when it is taking off with new and innovative business.

I look forward to hearing more, especially about any breakthroughs regarding the water reader invention.

As always, I am,
Affectionately your father,
Victor

As he sat to meditate that evening, Sasha said a prayer of thanks for this man who offered so much expert advice to him so freely. Would he have made it this far without Victor's help? Surely, just the feeling of having someone to talk to and to whom he could bring his problems was in itself invaluable. He was so grateful to have found not only a teacher but also, a friend. Tomorrow, he would order a DNA test for himself. Whatever the results, he already knew that his bond with Victor was a lasting one.

He lay down and closed his eyes for some much-needed sleep. Just as he drifted away, the thought crossed his mind, "I forgot to call Julia." He sat up, fighting the fleeting thought that he should just sleep and deal with his lapse in the morning. No. Small, invisible fingers of kindness hold together two people in the furies of life. He had the image burned into his mind as a boy of millions of small invisible fingers holding two people together as they traveled through a hurricane. He had often asked his mother, "What do the fingers look like?" "Are they yellow?" "Are they like earthworms?"

"They are invisible, like air," she told him once. "No one sees them except the other person and God."

"What do they feel like? Grass?" She sat down on the ground then and took him into her lap, wrapping her arms around him.

"They feel like this."

He texted Julia, "I'm sorry I did not call you as I said I would. I will call you . . . soon." Here he paused. Why pin himself down, after all?

This argument was a losing battle, however. He already knew the answer to that question, "How would I like to be treated?" He deleted the word *soon* and completed his text with the promise "tomorrow around 5 PM."

He sighed and lay back down. Just as he did, he heard the familiar beep and opened one eye to see a new text from Julia,

"In France. Long story. Got 'discovered' Tell you more tomorrow." He grinned, closed his eyes and disappeared into golden rest.

Chapter 7

Here's a New Way of Being Citizens

The Master said, "If your conduct is determined solely by considerations of profit you will arouse great resentment."
—Confucius

With only four or five days a month to focus on his experiments, Sasha became extremely conscious of the cost of his time. If he had three hours to spend in the lab, this was worth a great deal to him. He worked out how much he was actually paying for the use of the lab and weighed it against the progress he was making. Having a personal profit and loss statement made Sasha acutely aware of his own behaviors. He analyzed his needs against his desires and realized that he wanted to live a life that was highly creative. He had a strong desire to make and build new things. This desire overshadowed his need for structure and predictability. He already planned to establish a microeconomic lending institution, and that would be a large creative project.

Still . . . this last letter from Victor had struck a chord with him. He must plan to be able to develop new enterprises. He could see that his interest in scientific processes was simply a means to an end. He could do science,

91

but there were many other activities he enjoyed more. His meeting with Jan and Marlena had awakened in him the realization that he was quite good at presenting things and inspiring people with new systems. "I guess I have that in common with Victor," he thought. All his life, Yusup, who was a dentist in China, had encouraged him to be a scientist, and he had not questioned that he was a scientist. Even when he majored in business at UT, he thought that he would work with a science-based business. Now, though, he saw that he enjoyed the role of the closer, the presenter, and the big picture person more than that of the lab man.

Sasha wasn't sure, but he was beginning to understand that the kinds of people he needed to hire first were processors and salespeople. "After all," he thought as he lay down his pen thoughtfully, "I am a poet." Poetry was a highly schematic, abstract art that brought big picture systems down to concrete relationships. "Bottom line," he laughed, "It's like I'm meeting myself."

Sasha's mind was so full of the new enterprises that he was launching both for himself and as a catalyst at Water Macro, he noticed that he was becoming absentminded.

As he moved through day after day, completing minute tasks and considering how to incrementally build something big, his mind seemed too crammed full to work properly. He knew that one false step could cause damage or danger to himself and others: either his co-workers or Al. How could he manage to do so many things at so many different levels and still be clear and calm in his mind? This was a part of running a business that he had not read about. He wondered what Victor would say. He knew that Yusup would advise him to use a stick chart. Yusup had a system for monitoring his own activities using sticks laid on a table-top in specific formations. He had created it himself after learning how to use an abacus. Every day, Sasha had watched him stare at the bamboo sticks and slowly move one and add another. He understood that Yusup needed to see his ideas and projections in concrete form. Money, government, and much of life were actually abstractions, after all. Agreements between people are abstractions. Sasha sighed. His head still felt too full.

The next morning was Saturday. He got up at dawn, performed yoga stretches, and decided to take a walk. Even though he meditated each morning and each evening, he could see that his mind and body needed both more exercise and more stillness. How could he create that balance in the midst of so much activity?

"I need more than just a monetary profit and loss statement," he thought. "I need an accounting to myself of what drains me, what energizes me. . . . Yes, just as Victor said, what I like or desire and what I need, just at a more personal level." It was at that moment that Sasha knew that he would always release financial gain and even the thrill of creating a new enterprise if it interfered with his personal priorities of health and stillness. "So, now I have integrity, health, and stillness all before money." The scientist in him wondered how this would play out. Would establishing priorities ultimately build more wealth and power or less? He knew that the answer was purely academic since he was going to follow his path, regardless. His feet led him back up the hill to the abandoned church and to the hidden nook where he liked to sit.

Ah . . . stillness. It seemed to Sasha that life had taken on three kinds of activity: planning, executing plans, and stillness. Planning included introspection, and executing plans included trial and error. Stillness required thought control, body control, and receptivity. Both Yusup and Nur had often spoken of being yin and then of being yang—of filling up the space with activity and thoughts and then of emptying the space in order to listen to the voice of God, the song of the soul. He sat praying and meditating for an hour in the beautiful courtyard with the white arches and pink hibiscus flowers.

As he stood to leave, he felt a pressing certainty steal into his mind. He wanted to publicly address, possibly answer, the question that Victor so often mentioned: How can a democracy and a capitalistic economy coexist in these times of globalization and massive concentrations of wealth and poverty? Sasha also wondered how a republic could resist the collective parasite of entertainment media.

Even though Hillary Clinton could and did obstruct and misuse power, those deeds were less damaging than her media connections, Sasha thought.

Other politicians, like Obama, worked to turn government into a Kafkaesque nightmare: long lines, unending forms and regulations, taxes, incompetent managers, wasteful budgets. This sort of suffocating government was a river that had flowed through civilizations for millennia. Above it hung heavy, dark buildings of condemnation, name calling, anger, shame, self-righteousness and . . . the suffering of the powerless.

The names, the countries, the failures changed from century to century, but these questions pressed upon them always, even more now with the birth of the squalling entertainment media that took its place at the table: "How can we avoid falling into the furious anger of the poor against the abuses of the rich, since this inevitably leads to an enlargement of government? How can we regain statesmanship and bury partisan bickering?" Sasha sighed and shook his head. It was the manipulation of the political process by entertainment professionals that really bothered him. The way that one candidate could monopolize an election because of a power goal made it harder for democracy to coexist with capitalism.

Then there was the manipulation of people through language. The Islamic State, for example had nothing to do with Islam. If Americans could tell the difference between a Christian and a member of the KKK, they should be able to tell the difference between a Muslim and a group hijacking the name "Islam." Maybe they could tell the difference, and they just wanted to have a vehicle for rage and exclusivity. After all, as the United States becomes more and more diverse, those people who mistakenly see the wealth and opportunity here as a finite pie, feel . . . robbed.

There is no pie; opportunity cannot be weighed or counted any more than imagination or hope can.

Sasha felt the wind from the sea against his face as he turned toward home. Why not discover a new way of being citizens? There had to be something fresh and different. Why not? When he was a little boy, about nine years old, he became fascinated by Big Foot. For months, he created elaborate charts that showed sightings of Big Foot. Yusup had laughed at him, telling him that Big Foot did not exist, but Nur said this was good for a child. If he could believe in something that other people did not, then he could discover new things. Sasha set his jaw firmly as he walked into the house. He would press his fingers into the sinews of democracy's heart, and he *would* discover something new.

When he got back to the house, he grabbed his backpack and headed to the city. The thought entered his mind, "You need to stay and work in the lab." He had worked in the lab for the past two Saturdays and had decided to take a break. On the train, he texted Suki, "Hey, I'm going to the park. If you want to meet up, let me know."

She replied, "I'm working on some paintings. Stop by on your way home if you want."

Sasha settled into the seat. Something wasn't quite right. He had a feeling of unease that he couldn't shake. He traced it back to the text. Sasha glanced at his phone, and his eye fell on the text from Julia several days ago. Hmm. Something was odd about that. What did she mean when she said that she had been "discovered"? She was in Europe? Sasha knew that Julia was a quiet, conservative young woman. He decided to call her. The phone rang and rang and then went to voicemail. Sasha hung up and texted her, "Julia, where are you?"

He did not receive a reply. He couldn't shake the feeling that something was wrong, and it was wrong with Julia, he was sure. Sasha didn't know her parents' phone number. He called her friend Cindy.

"Hello?"

"Cindy, hi. It's Sasha."

"Hi Sasha. What's up?"

"I'm trying to get hold of Julia, and she's not picking up. Do you know where she is?"

"I know that she said she was going to Paris to possibly sign up with a talent agency to do some TV work and modeling."

"That's sort of weird. She never mentioned wanting to be a model or actress."

"I know, but she met this guy at a party and he said he could get her some gigs all over the world, and she did want to travel."

"Have you heard from her since she left?"

"No. I called, but she didn't call me back."

"Would you mind calling her parents for me and finding out if she's OK?"

"Sure." They hung up, and Sasha got off the train and walked up to the park. He watched the soccer players and bought a cone of fried calamari from a harbor vendor. The peaceful scene did not reassure him. When he came to an empty bench, Sasha lowered his backpack and took out a pen and paper. He was going to write back to Victor.

"Dear Victor . . ." His phone rang. It was Julia's father. He was quite upset. He had called his congressman. He had called the Japanese Embassy and the American Embassy in France. Sasha could hear Julia's mother speaking in rapid Japanese in the background. Basically, once Julia had reached France, they had not received any communication from her. Sasha's heart sank. He closed his eyes, and then he answered Mr. Sakari. "Sir, I suggest that you contact the FBI. In the meantime, I'll see if I can find something out. I'll call you back in an hour."

Suddenly, his phone beeped. He had a text from a number he did not recognize. It looked like gibberish to Sasha. Then, he recalled his "training" in the Numbers. The Numbers was a group of his middle-school friends. They were all immigrants from Asia except for Joseph, a second-generation Armenian boy. At first, the group was just about solving math problems and finding unexplained phenomena (like Big Foot) to discuss and argue about. As they grew older, however, the boys quickly discovered computer science and espionage. From the beginning, they had been captivated by the idea of spying, adventures, saving people, and using technology to escape from sci-fi monsters.

During college, the group met often. (Typical geeks, they had no social life.) They worked together to crack more and more difficult encryption devices. Eventually, they achieved complete access to any and all systems. This frightened and concerned them. As graduation neared, the Numbers group met and had one final discussion. Realizing the issues involved, they decided not to stay in touch and to refrain from hacking. The exception was any sort of personal or international emergency that a member might find himself in that the others could help with. In that case, they could reach each other through a special process.

The text that looked like gibberish was actually just phonetic Japanese. He quickly translated it: "I'm kidnapped. On a ship in France. Many others. Please help. Julia."

Sasha pulled out his iPad and, drilling down to the operating system, sent out the special, untraceable, SOS message, unreadable to all except a Numbers member.

He formulated his problem and question and sent that out quickly following the SOS. "Trace this number. Need latitude and longitude. Need video line. Names and background. Critical."

Within 15 minutes, Sasha saw a line of an encrypted message appear on his Mac. He decrypted the information and then used his Wi-Fi connection to grab the video feed. He found himself looking at a large yacht with waving banners two miles off the coast of Saint Tropez, France.

Sasha considered what to do next. He could turn this over to the FBI and the French police, and he would. But first, he called Victor's phone number, which he had looked up long ago. The voice that answered the phone sounded familiar. "That's odd," he thought, but he didn't have a second to spare.

"Victor, it's Sasha."

"Hello!"

"I've got an emergency. Can you give me an email address or text or fax where I can send you some data?"

"What's the problem?"

"My friend Julia's been kidnapped along with some other women. They're being held on a yacht off the coast of France."

"Ah. OK. Encrypt and send to . . ." Victor gave him an email address to his private server. "I'll see what I can do over here. Let the police in France know. Here's the phone number and name of an officer you should call. . . ."

They hung up quickly, and Sasha sent Victor an email and called the officer. He spoke to the man in French and told him what he knew.

Finally, he called Julia's parents. He explained to them what was happening. They began to weep. Sasha also felt close to tears as he spoke with them. He promised he would call them back within the next 30 minutes.

Watching the web video of the ship out at sea, he wondered what it was like for the women held there. Were they bound? Were they in darkness? Were they being beaten or raped? His heart ached for his friend.

As he watched the video, he noticed a large cruise ship enter the harbor and anchor about six miles out, blocking most of the access to open sea. Then, he observed a fishing ship fill up with tourists and begin a slow but steady advance out toward the yacht. It passed the yacht within 400 feet and continued to the nearby cliffs where the nude bathers were a popular sight.

Time passed. Sasha prayed and sent Julia his love. After half an hour, he called her parents to say that there was no change. They waited. The sun hit high noon in France, and Victor noticed that the yacht appeared to be pulling up anchor. Suddenly, it moved toward the open sea. As it picked up speed, three French police vessels appeared from behind the cruise ship. He saw blasts of fire from both sides, then police boarded and took possession of the craft. The police boats escorted the yacht to a mooring alongside the large ship. His heart leaped with joy as, in the glaring sunlight, he made out the forms of young women being assisted aboard and the forms of three men being moved to another one of the police vessels. Sasha saw that medical personnel from the ship were having one woman lifted on a stretcher.

He called Julia's parents. "She's been rescued," he told them, tears coursing down his face, "but I can't tell you if she is well or even if she is alive." They remained very quiet for about 20 seconds. Finally, her father spoke: "Sasha, we owe you our gratitude for your help. Please accept our thanks."

Sasha realized that this was a formal moment, "I gladly accept your thanks, Mr. and Mrs. Sakari. I am honored to be of service to you and to Julia. The French Coast Guard, the Maritime Gendarmerie, will be calling you any minute. I will get off the line."

Victor called him right after he got off the phone with the Sakaris and said, "All's well."

"Yes. Thanks for your help."

"Certainly. It's . . . it's nice to hear your voice."

"Yours too. It seems familiar to me, but I can't place it."

"I was surprised to get a call. I was expecting a letter."

"Yes, I enjoy writing the letters because it allows me to investigate my own thoughts. Also, I usually write them late at night, when it would be difficult to talk on the phone."

"Are you still going to write to me?"

"Yes."

"Great. By the way, great spy work. How did you manage to locate your friend?"

Sasha smiled and said, "Ah, well . . . let's just say, we all have our secrets."

Victor chuckled. "We'll have to tell your mother about this. She will be proud."

Sasha's heart leaped. "We?" he said. "How can we tell her? What do you mean? Do you know where she is?"

"Whoa! Hang on there. No, I don't know where she is. I have a suspicion of where she is. I expect that we—yes we—will find her when she is ready to be found. Don't you?"

Sasha relaxed. "Yes." He sighed. "My mother has her own reasons and her own life. That being said, I do want to see her and talk to her *and* I will find her before too long." He paused, suddenly sure of this, saying, "No matter what."

"I know you will, Sasha. For now, why don't you focus on recovering from today's drama and send me a letter, OK?"

"Yes, sir."

They said goodbye, and Sasha walked back to the train. This had been an unexpected sort of Saturday afternoon. He resisted the urge to call his Numbers friends. That would be breaking the agreement. Still, he wanted to say thanks. He found a picture of the Chinese character representing héng—relationship—and he put it on his Facebook page with public access. That was as much as he could do to say thanks.

Used with permission: Han Trainer Pro.

As the train pulled into the stop and Sasha boarded, he thought of Julia. He loved her. Not as a boyfriend, but as a dear friend. She was also his sister, like Suki. Perhaps he was not meant to fall in love in this life. He shrugged and started his letter to Victor as soon as he found a seat.

Dear Victor,

Thank you again for your assistance. I know you worked in the Russian Navy for a while, and being involved in a maritime operation must have been like meeting an old friend.

I really don't know the particulars of what happened, but it seems that Julia was taken into some sort of trafficking operation. When I know more, I will pass it on to you . . . with her permission.

So many things have been running through my head lately! I feel as if my brain is going to explode.

First of all, I'm close to putting my first prototype through final lab tests. It may fail. I've had six possible prototypes fail, but that's the nature of . . . well, everything really, isn't it?

I've become pretty philosophical. Yes, I see the way that in the U.S. political arena, many voters are confused. They think that they are suffering because of abuses by the wealthiest Americans when, in reality, they are suffering because our government has spent trillions of dollars more than it has to spend. We are in debt. Even though the economy has only grown by about 1%, corporations have lots of money. They're just sitting on it instead of hiring new people or investing in innovations. Why? Fear, I think. Even regular folks, thinking that the economy is struggling, are spending less.

All around us, it seems that people are getting the wrong information and drawing false conclusions. This concerns me. I wonder if there cannot be a way to create more dialogue—real dialogue, not media or virtual dialogue. I wonder if, just like with the old, crumbling, ineffective corporate operating model, we cannot find a more flat, more communicative citizenship model. I've been thinking about it quite a lot, but I want to know what you think of the idea. Can we start a movement—a sort of salon, brainstorming-type movement where people of all sorts of ideologies come together? Well, I want to experiment. I want to try it using Al's house. I think that I can obtain ownership of that house for almost nothing. I can use it as a gathering place for these "salons" I'm talking about.

At work, I've been able to talk very honestly with the employees so that they are now willing to openly share their opinions. Whew. It was not easy. It was really hard. I can't even begin to describe the pain and fear these people were carrying around. Just writing to you lifts some of the burden from my heart. Victor, some of my colleagues are from Greece and Venezuela, where the political regimes made promises and gave things away without figuring out how to pay for them. Money ran out to pay for all those free goods. Now there are great shortages, and the populace suffers. Spend more than you take in, and the day of recognizing that reality will come with a vengeance.

Well, let me move on before I become depressed. I found that by using humor, literally by acting—pretending to be one of the bosses, Jan or Marlena—this semi-mocking, semi-representation of the authority figures loosened them up tremendously. They just relaxed more than I've ever seen them whenever I put on my "act." While they are laughing, I get them to form groups and begin to engage in brainstorming. The first few times, they did it thinking it was a game of some kind. Finally, they realized that this was going to be part of their jobs. They did freeze up a little bit, but overall, things are definitely going better than I had hoped. I'm almost certain that Water Macro will umbrella my new company—that is, if they agree to my terms and if I can present a working prototype.

I don't know if I mentioned it to you, but I spoke with Yusup, my . . . first father, the other day. We just talked casually. It was good closure for me. He was friendly and invited me to come visit whenever I wanted to. I told him how his toddler son had accidently called me on their land line and then made gurgling baby sounds. He enjoyed that, and we had a good laugh. The little boy's name is James, so Jimmy. I think of him as my little brother, Jimmy.

So, ending with what I started with, Victor, profit and loss. Your encouragement to go forward in life with a personal profit and loss statement really hit home. I've been taking the idea into time itself and thoughts themselves. How much do I gain in life by spending time away from work? How much do I gain in wealth by turning my thoughts away from building it on a regular basis? I want to move math into the realm of the heart and the mind. (LOL. This reminds me of a popular book Suki is reading, Heart Math.*)*

This sort of profit and loss naturally leads one to ask, "How do I share, give away my time and money and have it be the most effective?" You see, Victor, you've opened a Pandora's box here. I bet you're going to wish you never mentioned profit and loss statement to me. . . .[smile].

It's been a long day . . .as you know. A hundred years ago, most people spent their days performing simple tasks within their community. Who would have dreamt that one day in our global society could include so many wide-ranging thoughts and even criminal and police warfare waged over 10,000 miles away?

I'm so worried about Julia. I don't even know if she is alive. How could this happen? Was I so wrapped up in my own pursuits that I neglected our friendship? Why didn't I call her back sooner? I'm plagued by these questions.

Talk to you soon.

Your son,

Sasha

That night, Sasha could not sleep. He could not read or write. As he cared for Al, his mind was like a wooden block. Between 3 and 4 AM, he made a caramel cake. He had never made a cake before, but he had decided to comfort himself, and cake was comfort.

When six o'clock struck, he found that Al was cranky and didn't want to walk. Picking the frail body up in his arms, he began to walk toward the bathroom. Al, his arm hooked around Sasha's neck, looked into his eyes. "Who has burned your rice?" he asked in a near whisper. "Was it the fighters from Kinman?" Sasha lowered him gently onto his shower chair.

"No, Lao [older friend], I am Sasha." He turned on the water. Someone had burned his rice field . . . in a way. Someone had taken a human being that he cared about and treated her as a thing: a thing.

In the days that followed, Sasha went about his work and experiments with the same feeling of woodenness. He ran a few brainstorming groups and even set up a meeting with Jan and Marlena two weeks out. Not wanting to disturb the Sakaris, Sasha finally called Suki and told her everything that had happened. She was concerned for his state of mind. "Listen Sasha, you're always so busy. Take a day off of everything. Call Julia's number and find out what's going on. Come over here any time you want, and I'll make you good food."

"Suki . . . I . . . don't think I'm going to take off work for this, but, yes, I will come over for lunch next Saturday or Sunday if that suits you."

"It's on my calendar for Sunday," she said, and he knew she was writing his name in four-inch block letters on her five-foot calendar made from an old front door and wallpaper.

That day on the train back home, Sasha texted Julia's number. "Julia?"

"Sasha?" His eyes jumped in his skull at the sight of her text.

"Yes. Where are you?"

"Home. Just got out of hospital."

"Are you OK?"

"No."

He called her immediately. "What's wrong?"

"I . . . I'm not sick. They didn't beat me up . . . or . . . ."

"What's going on? What happened?"

"Sasha, I just fell for an old trick. They trapped me in an apartment once I got to France with ten other women. Then, they put us on the yacht. We were in a small space for many days without food or water. We could hear our captors negotiating business deals for us. We were something they were selling. They were selling us. I was the most valuable because I'm Japanese." She sobbed and then caught herself. "I was so stupid. Why? Why did I go there? Why?"

"It's no use beating yourself up, Julia. I've been doing that. I should have stayed in touch with you better. I'm so sorry I wasn't there for you."

"Sasha. No. I was so headstrong. I was naïve. My mother tried to talk me out of going, but I was certain that I would be traveling the world and sending her postcards. Can you believe it? I didn't even run a background check on the guy who offered me the contract."

"Jean-Paul."

"You know his name?"

"I had to find out everything in order to find you."

"How? How did you find me?"

Sasha sighed. "Julia, I used some computer hacking skills. Please don't ask me anything else, OK?"

"OK . . . thank you."

"You're welcome. You're my friend. I would do anything to help you."

"Sasha?"

"Yes?"

"I don't know what to do now. I'm back home. I graduated. I could look for a job, but I feel so weird."

"Like how?"

"Like...like I want to be different than I was. I want to change."

"How?"

"I have no idea, but I am not afraid anymore of being different. That is one change that can lead to others."

"Well, how can I help you in your change?"

"Can I come see you?"

Sasha paused and she understood his hesitancy. "No. I mean just to be in a new place. I wouldn't need to stay with you. I know we're platonic."

"Come whenever you want. Actually, come and help me. I'm starting a salon, a political and social brainstorming session for United States citizens."

She laughed a hearty laugh that warmed his heart. "Really? Wow. That's . . . cool. He knew she was reacting to how out of character such a bold move would have been for him while they were in college. She added quickly, "I'll help."

"OK. Let's stay in touch. Let's talk next Saturday morning."

"Yes. Thank you, Sasha. Talk to you soon. Goodbye."

Finally, finally, Sasha leaned back on the train seat, sending gratitude to God for preserving Julia's life.

Government proved to be a necessity when it came to crime. The U.S. military had been reduced dramatically, he knew. Was that wise? Wouldn't the same sort of criminal mind that kidnapped and sold young people plot to war against America? Were they prepared to defend their freedoms? He didn't know but he wanted to find out. He was beginning to feel powerful. He felt in that moment, as the train slipped into the Arapaho Center station, that he could do whatever he put his mind to. He was a force, a real force. When he stepped off the train, his foot landed on the ground with more weight. He walked knowing that he could make a difference and that he would.

Back at the lab, Sasha checked his equipment before going upstairs to fix Al's dinner. Just as he was heating up fish head soup, the doorbell rang. He saw a white-haired man standing on the porch, a fellow who looked a lot like Santa. "Crandall!" He flung open the door and embraced his old friend, who grinned at him sheepishly.

Sasha grabbed his hand and pulled him into the kitchen to meet Al. "Al, look who came to visit me!" Al looked up without surprise at Crandall and nodded. He was waiting for his soup. Sasha quickly brought the bowl to him and tucked in his napkin.

"Crandall, how did you find me? Did my publisher give you my address here? I asked them to send a book to you in London, but I didn't know if you were still there. This is so great!"

Crandall smiled gleefully but said nothing. He was being unusually quiet, Sasha thought. "Did you read my book?"

Crandall nodded and said, "Yes, I did. I found it wonderful."

"What was wonderful about it?" Sasha's heart leaped at the joy of sharing time with his London friend.

"The way that you were so vulnerable was wonderful. It's a rare man who can expose his heart the way you do in those poems, Sasha. Also, though, your use of the English language shows a keen understanding of spiritual symbolism and a regional syntax."

Sasha nodded. He loved analytical literary talk. "I just can't believe you're sitting here in the kitchen with me and Al. It's so . . . otherworldly. I haven't had a chance to tell you, but I've had a difficult week. I almost lost a good friend to violence."

Crandall nodded. He was looking down at the floor. Sasha wiped Al's mouth and put his walker in front of him. He asked Crandall, "Do you mind waiting until I've put on his PJs and gotten him into bed?"

"No. Not at all. Do you mind if I look around this palace?" Crandall glanced appreciatively at the vast spaces around him.

"Go for it. My lab is in the basement." Sasha walked toward the bedroom suite behind Al's shuffling gait.

Crandall watched him closely as he passed. "You're not wearing your hat."

"No. I stopped wearing it." Sasha smiled, almost embarrassed that he was so comfortable with his red hair.

"I like it. You look great. . . . OK. I'm taking a self-guided tour. I will see you in . . .half an hour."

Sasha nodded and focused on lifting the walker over a step.

When he returned to the dining area, Crandall handed him a mug of hot tea. "Don't you have to stay with him?"

Sasha nodded. "Well, I have about an hour before his medication wears off. It makes him sleep heavily. I'll just sit up here where I can see and hear him, though." Sasha moved a chair over to the pink marble landing leading into Al's bedroom suite, took a sip of his tea, and looked at Crandall expectantly.

"Before we go any further," Crandall said, putting his cup down and walking closer to Sasha, "I need to tell you something."

"What?"

Crandall didn't say anything, he just stood in front of Sasha quietly. Then, he reached into his wallet and pulled out an old Polaroid and handed it to Sasha wordlessly.

Sasha took the picture. It was a photo of a 30-something young man wearing a green sweater. He had a full head of red hair and was standing in front of a sign that said "circus" in Russian. Sasha looked at the picture, the same picture he had tucked into his haiku book that he knew was a picture of his father, Victor. He stared at Crandall. "You're Victor."

Crandall nodded. "I'm Victor. I know, I know you may be feeling that I have tricked you, Sasha. Well, I did trick you, but not, not to hurt you."

"Why?" Sasha shook his head. "I'm so confused. I have two different relationships, two important relationships and they're *with the same person?*"

Crandall/Victor swallowed, sighed, and nodded. He sat down. "We . . . your mother and I . . . we wanted to . . ."

"You and my mom came up with this?"

Crandall/Victor nodded.

"Yes, you see . . . . Look, you were just leaving Yusup after their marriage broke up. You were alone in a cold, dark winter in a strange city. Your mother was concerned that you were too isolated. All along, I had planned to contact you via letter and gradually get to know you so that you could accept me or not accept me as your father." Sasha nodded. So far, this made sense.

"So . . . all of that plan was in place and agreed-upon. Then, suddenly, Bo . . . Bo Nur . . . contacted me again. She was insistent that I befriend you sooner. She was really concerned about your mental state. I didn't want to force myself on you as your father. I felt that it was not fair to you. Finally, we agreed that I would be a friendly old soul that you met in your late-night wanderings. I would be there for you to just hang out with and feel safe in home-like surroundings. That's what she wanted. She is first and foremost a mother, Sasha. Even though she left your dad . . . Yusup, she always kept an eye on you. This way, we figured that if you didn't accept Victor—me—as your father, Crandall could gradually fade away too."

Sasha nodded. "OK." He sighed. "I see that it makes sense in a crazy two-spies-for-parents kind of way."

"You do?"

"Yes, I do. I understand." He stared at the floor contemplatively. "She was right, of course. I was too alone and depressed in a strange city. I did need a friend just like Crandall," he mused. "You know what? I'm realizing that you, Victor, are actually a lot more mellow than I thought you were."

Victor smiled and said, "I am?"

"Yeah. I mean, I was thinking of you as being a pretty strict sort of business guy, but now I see that you are someone who enjoys the arts and can tell a mean story."

Victor cleared his throat and said, "Hmm, good to know."

Sasha stood up suddenly. "Let me hug you again. Now that I know that you're my father."

The two men embraced, and Victor wiped a tear from his eye. "Excuse me. We Russians weep."

"I only have a little while left, Victor. Tell me, what did you think of my last letter?"

Victor blew his nose and gathered himself. "I think, Sasha, that being a citizen in a democracy is a lot like being a husband. You must be willing to admit you are wrong freely and often. You must learn to listen very carefully, and you must invent, invent, invent, always being creative and curious. That is the only way to be happy for a long time with someone you love. So, if you want to invent a new way for citizens to communicate with one another about their government and society, then I say, go for it."

Sasha smiled.

"Keep this in mind. The United States of America spends trillions of dollars more than it has. We are deeply in debt and behaving as if we are not. Above all else, we must focus on being a nation that is fiscally responsible. I say, 'above all else' because if we cannot operate according to the monies that we actually have, we cannot address with integrity any other issue, including racism, poverty, environmental upheaval, and crime. Part of operating with fiscal responsibility is limiting the reach of government. So, there is a two-fold reason to limit government—three, really, if you consider that it is a litmus test of our integrity as well."

"But . . .," Sasha said as he looked into his mug like a fortuneteller. "What about Occupy Wall Street? I mean, OK, we need to be fiscally responsible—especially the government. Look at the private sector, the banks. There's fraud and cashing in on the little guy."

Victor nodded. "Yes and no. A Federal Court of Appeals has overturned penalties against Bank of America and an operator with Countrywide Mortgage. It looks on the outside that there was this fraud, but what really happened when bad mortgages were oversold and the housing market went bust is a combination of poor policy, poor incentives, and a craze for residential real estate that came just as much from the seller as the buyer. People like to use the words 'fraud' and 'greed.' You were talking about how ISIS misuses the term 'Islam.' Well, it works both ways. If you really want to drill down to the truth, then you can't be afraid to say that the bankers aren't to be blamed."

Sasha leaned back in his chair. He got up and walked into the kitchen. "Hey, do you want some cake?"

Victor nodded, "I could eat cake." Sasha cut them both big pieces of cake. "This is *my* cake. I made it late last night when I couldn't sleep. I hope you like yellow cake and caramel icing."

"I do like it. Have you ever tried a cake called Hummingbird cake?"

"No."

"It's great."

Sasha set a large piece of the triple-layer cake down in front of Victor. "Here you go."

Their eyes met in complete trust. Victor stuck a fork into the mountain of yellow confection. "Let the party begin!"

Chapter 8

Profit Picture® Illuminates

Without measurement, there can be no satisfying progress. For progress to be measurable, one or two things must be true. Either something is achieved that can be counted with numbers, or something is achieved that is a clear milestone—it either happens or it does not.

—**Dan Sullivan**, The Strategic Coach®

O ver their heads, in the low-ceilinged lab, the workers at Water Macro could hear the thunder cracking the sky like a painted vase. The lights flickered and went out for a minute. They flinched and kept on identifying bacteria, filtering minerals, adding oxygen, and testing activity. Water had a life of its own. You could test it, treat it, roll it, and burn it, but the best way to tell if it was pure was to drink it . . . well, to let a living organism drink it. They kept human cells of all kinds on hand for final tests.

Sasha had learned a great deal at Water Macro. He had spent almost a hundred hours reading posts and papers from leading scientists on recent experiments. This had helped him plan his own research very carefully and document dozens of actions and reactions he would not have been aware of otherwise. Ah, science.

Science was everything. Music, dance, accounting, computers, physics, yoga, birth, and death were all part of science. He loved science. Poetry was a science.

Sasha remembered his mother saying, "You do not attract what you want, you attract who you are." What kind of science was this? String theory, of course. OK. But what was at the heart of a string, or "resonating object points"? He knew the answer because his mother had told him: "Thought." "Thought," Nur said to him many times as he struggled to get what he wanted or accept that he had not, "thought is everything. You are a thought in the Mind of God. All matter is. When you are sad, Sasha, you must find the sad thought like a little fish in the pond. You find it, and you catch it. Then, you pull out of your bucket a beautiful rainbow fish and you put it in the pond instead. That is your positive thought."

She had gently and firmly taken him through the exercise many times. He laughed, remembering clearly that his bad thought when his father refused to allow him to have a dog was, "He is not fair to me."

They worked on this one for about three weeks. Just when he was helping set the table or chopping up the onions she would ask him, "Do you have a good thought yet?"

"I don't have a dog, and I wish I had one. Chichi is mean," he said. And then, "I would be a good dog owner."

"That one is a little bit better," she said. "Why would you be a good dog owner?"

"I could love it."

"How?"

"Play with it."

"What else?"

"Feed it, walk it, wash it, help pay for its shots and food."

"Is there any way you can love a dog without owning it at your house?"

He looked at his mother, startled. Their family, their apartment, was their entire world. They did not venture out of it once they came back from work and school. Neither of his parents were members of any group, nor did they join in community activities. What was she saying?

"There is an animal shelter behind the drug store. They need volunteers."

With her help, he had gone to the shelter and become a volunteer. It was much more satisfying to play with 40 dogs than with 1. He learned that he did not know his mother as well as he thought he did. Now, looking back, he could see many signs that she was not the quiet, narrow housewife. She put cut-out pictures from magazines of great works of art on the fridge: Modigliani, Cezanne, Sargent, and Picasso. She played music from many different countries—Merle Haggard, Enya, Ragas, Peruvian folk songs, Bach.

Sasha remembered how Yusup would look at her with a perplexed expression on his face, and she would bow her small head and stir the soup, clean the floor. One evening, however, he remembered she was very excited and exuberant, even. She had a DVD of a Chinese comedian. The fellow was making fun of Chinese people, and he was spot on. His mother laughed a little and then more, then she just laughed until tears poured down her cheeks. Both Yusup and Sasha had watched her with some alarm. They chuckled, too, at first and enjoyed the way he mocked the over-serious expressions and the over-concern with eating certain foods. Mostly, though, they slowly absorbed the idea that this woman was a stranger. She had secret thoughts and feelings, surely she did; after all, they'd never witnessed her mocking her own race before.

It wasn't just the Han Chinese ethnic group that the comedian mentioned. He held the Uyghur, the Turkish/Chinese ethnic group to which Yusup belonged, up for jest too, even putting on a traditional Uyghur hat and doing one of the dances in a funny way. Yusup did not like this. He pushed the eject button, took the DVD, and put it away. Then, to show he was a thoughtful and caring husband, he put in a DVD of the popular 1991 Chinese movie "Raise the Red Lantern." Nur became very quiet. They were at war, as parents sometimes are.

Part of his mother's training of Sasha was her example. Whenever she entered into conflict, she would follow a pattern that none of his friends' mothers followed. When they found themselves disagreeing with their husbands, they would bow and leave the room. Then, they would make cold, tasteless dinners or accidently let the cat into the bedroom or some such thing. Nur, on the other hand, had a sort of script that she followed as if in school. First, she would turn to the person, usually Yusup but sometimes Sasha or her friend Li Li and say what she observed. The time Yusup took the comedy DVD, out she said, "I see that you have removed my DVD before it was over without asking me." Yusup nodded. He was used to it. He muttered, "I do not need to ask you."

Next, she would say how that action affected her. She said, "When you removed that DVD without asking me, I felt that you did not care about me."

Finally, they had learned, she would make a request. While Yusup could ignore this last part, Sasha could not. He always paid attention to the request.

"My request is that you return the DVD to the TV and that you ask me before you remove it."

At this, Yusup had laid down on the floor with his face down and toward her. She saw that he was making fun of her by pretending to worship her. She quietly got up and left the room and began making lunches for the next day.

Sasha saw each time that his mother was not angry or upset. That she did not allow Yusup to bother her. Even as a child, he knew that almost everything she did was for him, to show him something, to tell him something secret .

That night, he heard her laugh and speak in a soft voice to Yusup. She was always kind to him, and he did not beat her. Perhaps he had tried once but soon realized that he could not beat her because she was a well-trained martial artist. So he did not try except for that last night she was with them. . . .

All of Sasha's friends' fathers beat their mothers. They spoke to him of this in shocked and horrified voices when they were young. As they grew older, they had to reconcile their love and their hatred for their fathers. In China around this time, in the 1990s, a law was passed that it was illegal for a man to beat his wife. Soon, the Chinese courts were so overwhelmed by cases brought by women against their husbands that the Chinese legal system came to a standstill. The law had to be rescinded.

Sasha wondered what it would have been like to grow up in the same house with Victor and Nur. Victor stayed with him at Al's house for a day. They played a game of chess. Victor showed him a business software system he had invented—a sort of computerized projection of how a business was doing and what it needed to do to improve, all in visual terms. He called it "Profit Picture." After looking at a few sample screenshots and getting the hang of it, Sasha decided he would pitch using Profit Picture to Jan and Marlena.

Being with Victor in person calmed Sasha down. Here was someone who was consistently showing up for him and who made the effort to reach out to him, which made Sasha feel great. It went a long way toward easing the turmoil in his mind when his mother left and Yusup started a new family.

Sasha had actually taken Victor up to the top of the hill and shown him the place he liked to sit and meditate. Victor loved it. "Where do you go to meditate?" Sasha asked him.

"I don't meditate," he answered smiling.

Sasha looked confused. "But I read a great deal about Christianity and even about the early church you described Stephen being a member of. Meditation appears to be a big part of Christianity. Isn't it? I read a book by Brother Lawrence, *Practicing the Presence of God*. This was mentioned so many times in my research of Christianity that I downloaded it and read it."

"Sasha, Christians did start out sitting together in silence to see the 'tongues of fire' or to hear the voice of God, but those are what we call 'the Mystics of the Church.' Today, most Christians don't meditate. We work with the poor and needy, we pray, and we study the scriptures . . . and we sing songs of praise."

"Oh," Sasha said. They walked along in silence, exploring the grounds of the abandoned church. Sasha tried to contain his disappointment. He had been drawn to Victor's and Suki's descriptions of the master, Jesus Christ, and he had, little by little, learned more and more until he felt certain that this was also his master. But . . . the core of his life was his still communion with God during meditation. Already, he had felt the presence of Jesus Christ in his twice daily meditations. What a great love had passed over him, like a wave, a giant wave of compassion and even a kind of sorrow. Deep down, Sasha had been hoping to share a short meditation with Victor in his favorite spot. They sat down and looked at a hibiscus flower, and Victor recited a poem by St. Ignatius:

Lord, teach me to be generous.
Teach me to serve You as You deserve;
to give and not to count the cost,
to fight and not to heed the wounds,
to toil and not to seek for rest,

to labor and not to ask for reward,
save that of knowing that I do Your will.

"Amen." Victor sat quietly looking at the hibiscus.

Sasha, added his own amen, except that it was, "Om."

Victor looked so quiet and happy. "What does 'Om' mean?" he asked with a childlike look.

"It is the name of the Holy Spirit. It is the life force that connects all of life and draws us unto God."

"Ah." Victor nodded. "Thank you. I'm learning new things from you, Sasha."

They started back to the house, walking briskly, and then they spontaneously broke into a run, racing like brothers. "Don't . . . let . . . me . . . win. . . ." Victor gasped as he sprinted ahead. Sasha passed him, slowed down, and then passed him again, laughing. Finally, he ran with him to the front door.

When they got inside, Victor sprawled across one of the curving pink couches, something Sasha had never had the nerve to do. "This is a great *place, Sasha*! It would make a perfect salon setting. You could even host . . . well . . . almost anything here: art shows, seminars, classes, jam sessions, you name it!" For the first time, Victor let a hint of a Russian accent enter his speech. He was feeling at home in this Oriental mansion.

"Yes. I've thought a lot about it. It would be quite a lot of work to keep it structured, manage bartering and donations, no actual payments, and mainly to reflect a consistent message in different types of media. It's two-pronged— the meetings and ideas and the dissemination of them through literature and other media."

Victor was watching him talk. His eyes were full of pride and happiness. "Do you know what Thomas Paine said? 'We have it in our power to begin the world again.'"

"Yes, that's what I'm doing."

Victor smiled. "Yes, it is."

Victor left that evening, and after closing the door behind him, Sasha felt satisfied. He had found his father—what a father! He still had hold of his first father, Yusup, whom, despite his faults, he loved. Life stretched before him.

He dreaded the next day's meeting with Jan and Marlena to discuss the restructuring of Water Macro's business operations. He had prepared a proposal for them, including illustrations, to underwrite his own venture. At Victor's suggestion, he had quickly applied for a host of patents, which were pending. Just in case they liked his idea too much. The patent fees had cut into his savings, but he put that thought out of his mind. Water could not be stopped. It was truth, and it flowed freely forward. So would he.

On Friday morning, just seven days after his first meeting with Marlena and Jan, Sasha sat, tie knot snug against his throat, in the Water Macro conference room. He projected his proposal onto the large screen in the conference room, and he had prepared hard copies of it to hand out, too. He'd reviewed the benefits of Profit Picture and had those ready to display, as well:

1. Develop a more collaborative relationship with team members because they can see visually the abstract realities of the business profit and loss cycles.
2. Set expectations for individuals that can be visually integrated into the company's projected plan so they can see exactly how their work affects the big picture.
3. Strengthen capital with funding a resource that rewards and retains key profit makers.
4. Monitor key market segments to determine if they are expanding, slipping, contracting, or improving—all within 10 seconds or less.
5. Integrate data across data sources.
6. Limit and eliminate talent poaching.

Right on time, Jan and Marlena came into the conference room and sat down. Their eyes were downcast, and they seemed very cool toward him. He decided to address this right away. "Good morning, Jan."

"Good morning." Jan did not look up.

"Good morning, Marlena."

"Hello." Marlena was clearly pissed off.

"Before we get started, is there anything you would like to talk to me about?" Sasha asked.

He sat down. He waited. He knew it was coming. The anger was palpable.

"Well," Marlena began, "since you asked. . . ."

"Yes?"

Jan shot out, "Apparently, you've been mocking us in front of the employees."

Marlena added, "Don't bother denying it. Someone caught you on camera and sent us the video."

Sasha took a deep breath. "I'm not going to deny it, exactly. I will say that I was not mocking you."

"What do you call it, then?" asked Jan.

"I call it impersonation, a comedy bit, a strategic way of breaking through the wall of fear. In other words, in no way was I implying that you are stupid or crazy. Instead, I was simply offering the employees a bit of comic relief. If you continue watching the video, you can see that once they feel relaxed and unafraid, your employees were able to participate in brainstorming sessions. You have benefited already from many of their ideas and suggestions."

Jan's body relaxed into her chair. Marlena shrugged, and he could see that she was getting over her anger. "But . . . why did you have to do it? Was this the only way?"

"Well, would you mind if I shared one of these employees' personal stories with you?"

The women nodded. "OK."

"Shru-lee, the woman who does all your auditing, came from mainland China. She worked in a large firm that processed medical labs. For twenty years, she worked for the company, and every week, her manager came into her office, randomly grabbed one of her files, and began screaming at her that she had been doing a bad job and would soon be on the street. In Communist China, if you are fired from a job, no one else will hire you. There, people can be fired for small details, such as forgetting to turn off the light when they leave or making too many copies and wasting paper.

"One day, the office had a special going away party for Shru-lee's manager, who was retiring. The big boss over the entire division came in with his secretary.

She held a large bunch of flowers to offer as his gift. The big boss saw Shru-lee standing nearby and told his secretary to give her the flowers. He told Shru-lee to find a vase in the kitchen area where they kept many vases and to put the flowers in a vase and put it in the center of the refreshment table.

"Shru-lee went into the kitchen and got out several vases. She stood there trying to decide which vase to use. If she chose a large vase, the bosses might criticize her for wasting water, and she might be fired. If she chose a small vase, she might be accused of making the flowers look bad. She considered cutting the flowers to fit them into a low, wide-mouthed vase, but she was afraid to do that. She actually never left the kitchen. When someone came into the kitchen about an hour later, they found her frozen with the flowers in her hand. She could not speak or move. She had had a nervous breakdown.

"The medics took her to the hospital. She lost her job. She lost her home. She and her mother went to the country to work in the fields. Her mother died. When this happened, her first cousin offered to let her come live with his old mother and take care of her in San Francisco. She found this job and has been coming in to work every single morning, seven days a week, at 7:30 AM and leaving at 7:30 PM. She also works all night, caring for the old woman.

"Shru-lee wears a diaper so that when she has to relieve herself and it is not her scheduled break, she can. Shru-lee had a breakdown in the kitchen at her Chinese job because she could not make a decision. Every decision she considered seemed to her to be too risky. As a worker in a Communist system, she had only been punished for speaking out and never encouraged to think for herself."

"Now, Shru-lee's story is similar to that of most of your workers. You, Jan and Marlena, are, in their minds, like soldiers, police, or bosses who will fire them at the drop of a hat. The fact that they can go out and get another job is not real to them. They are terrified of falling into desperate poverty and even death at the slightest misstep. So, in such a tight, hierarchical structure that you have set up at Water Macro and with such traumatized individuals afraid of thinking for themselves, there was no way to get them to relax and realize that you were not so rigid, and that you could laugh at yourselves—except by doing impersonations. You can laugh at yourselves, can't you? If you want to encourage free thinkers and imaginative input, you have to leave your egos at the door. A flat hierarchy just can't survive generals."

Sasha felt quite on edge after delivering this speech. He had prepared to deliver it, however. When change occurs in a business, someone has to let go of some of the control, and it is usually the bosses.

Jan and Marlena seemed relieved to have a way to move past being mad at him. Jan sighed and said, "I know that the whip-cracking factory owner doesn't look that different from the whip-cracking slave owner. I grew up with that model. My parents ran a sugar company in Savannah, and that's how they ran it. I guess I've replicated it here, except with Asians instead of African Americans. I've felt pretty guilty, but at the same time, no one complained, and we kept a steady profit margin."

"So, you felt guilty and you observed that your employees were unhappy, plus you knew from your experiences as a child that it was not the best way to go," Sasha reflected back to Jan.

"Yes. Yes. All of that is true. Look," she sighed heavily, "I can see how you are just doing a comedy act. You're really just giving them instructions, but as if you're me or Marlena."

"Right. I'm actually telling them how to get into groups and what to analyze for the brainstorming session."

"Yeah." Marlena leaned back in her swivel chair. "Yeah. We've been too hard on these guys. If we want to reap the benefits of their expertise, we have to let them know that we've changed and we're not going to hurt them if they criticize how we've been doing things. So . . . . Show me your impersonation of me." She grinned at Sasha.

Sasha stood up, flipped an imaginary long, blond curl over his shoulder and said in a Texas twang, "Y'all be quiet now and listen up. I'm goin' to be puttin' you in five groups. You three in the corner and you three on this table are in Group One. Anyone who doesn't want to can wrestle me."

Marlena laughed, and Jan eagerly jumped in, "OK. OK. We have to be serious. That was a really good job, Sasha. Don't show me how you do me. The next time you stand in front of the employees, let me know, and I'll show up and impersonate *you*. That way, they'll know that we are really open and listening." Everyone laughed.

Sasha nodded. "I'm so glad you were willing to communicate your concerns to me openly. Are you both ready to begin the presentation?"

They nodded, and he started the slide show. On the wide screen appeared the words "Profit Picture."

Then, Sasha displayed a colorful graph that highlighted the strengths and weaknesses of Water Macro, touching on turnover, sales, manufacturing costs, and losses. As he spoke and moved from slide to slide, he could hear the two women exchanging notes and observations. They were most impressed that all of the company's data had been integrated into a big picture. They were even more impressed that the causes and effects of various marketing and operational decisions were represented in such a way that they could be mapped to profits and losses.

Sasha pointed out as he went through the slides, "If it is a measureable event in your operations, Profit Picture captures it and presents it in the form of a visual. The point of Profit Picture is to help people who are visual learners see things more perfectly. The website is www.profitpicture.net."

Executive Compensation Dashboard:
Retain and Reward Key Profit Contributors

Am I On Track?

What Has My Performance Been?

Take Note!

What Amount Is Projected at My Retirement?

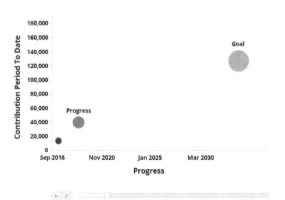

This report supports your executive compensation plan. Each participant has access to this report. The meter in the upper left part of the screen shows how the individual is performing to goal. The needle points to where the participant is today (in this case, at 150% of the goal).

To the right of the meter is a bar chart. This visual may vary from the sample depending on the parameters of the plan for each company. In our example, two components make up the bonus calculation: the bar meaning revenue shown on the left axis and the dot meaning net income increase shown as percentage on the right axis. The line connecting the dots aligns with the vertical axis on the right (percentage). The shaded area marked "N" for net income is the share for the selected executive.

The box in the lower left corner of the screen offers a "notes" place for short-term goals with this individual to keep them on track. This is a place for quick notes about accountability references.

The lower right portion of the report is specific to the participant. In our sample, the dots represent what may happen in the future based on company performance and board discretion over the plan. In this design, the largest dot represents a retirement goal. The goals are subject to change due to company and participant performance and are not guaranteed. The smallest dot represents what has been set aside today for the future. The dot labeled "Progress" shows the projected amount by a certain month along the executive's timeline (i.e., November 2018).

This report can serve as an excellent management tool for the owner and a powerful incentive for the participant.

Labor Productivity Dashboard

This chart overlays current month data over a rolling 12 months of data. The darker bar shows a rolling 12 months, and the lighter bar shows the most recent month. While this might be a new way for you to look at data, think about the valuable information it provides: You get to see labor productivity for the current month compared with trend data. Are you up/down/even? If there's no current month data, you'll want to look at why there were no sales in that category. If the light bar is significantly shorter than the darker bar, you should look at what's going on there. If the light bar is higher, then congratulations may be in order. Is your training paying off? Is there a new client in that area? This chart can be very helpful for professionals who bill by the hour.

This report is customizable by category and time frame so that you can focus on specific results when you're counseling a particular department, rather than showing

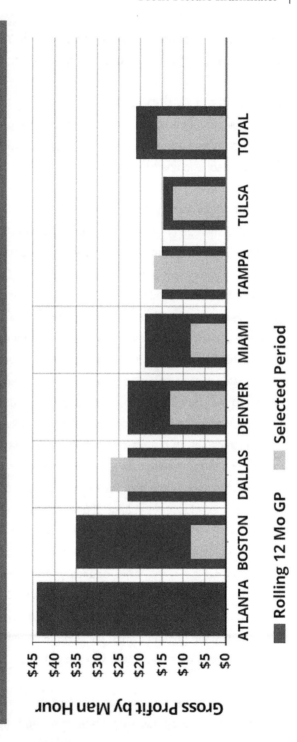

all the results. Specific cities are used in the demonstration. You can use any common reference for comparison, such as product, territory, region, or salesperson.

Revenue and Profit Dashboard

This is a powerful overview with four visuals of sales revenue and profit trends based on data pulled nightly from existing sources. You can see trends immediately without having to train someone to analyze this for you.

1. **Revenue Goal Meter**: Using your sales data for the revenue goal for the trailing 12 months (T12M) as compared with your sales goals (budget) by division, you can quickly see which division is contributing to your progress and which ones are lagging. You can specify data by division or by location and roll them up to Total Company relative to goals.

2. **Profit Variance**: This view shows the current profit trend for T12M compared with the underlying gray area for the prior 12 months. Data come from net income booked and show in a highly visual way how things are going, by the same categories as specified above, with a company rollup.

3. **Backlog**: As you think about sales and profit trends in graphs 1 and 2, you may be wondering what's coming along to be billed, that is, reassurance that business is on the way. In this example, the current backlog shows you the up-to-the-minute data available from your systems while comparing T14M to the prior 14 months. Data come from the contract amount for jobs, including the addition of change orders minus billed amount to determine the backlog. All data come from your existing systems. The backlog visual shows the highest five-year backlog in the upper boundary and the worst five-year backlog in the lower boundary. The dark, solid line reports the previous 14 months; the lighter, dashed line shows the current 14 months. Being able to quickly see trends from four data points at once is important; you can see the best and worst backlog points and where you were at the same time last year and where you are right now. See issues before they become big problems.

4. **Profit Net Income %**: This visual shows performance of net income as a percentage (horizontal axis). Data come from the general ledger. The

Profit Picture

REVENUE AND PROFIT (BY DEPT)

ATLANTA

Revenue Goal

$710,941

Backlog

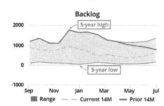

Profit Variance

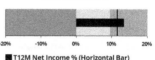

◇ T12M ◢◢ Goal

Profit Net Income %

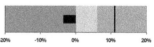

■ T12M Net Income % (Horizontal Bar)
— Prior T12M Net Income % (Vertical Bar)

BOSTON

Revenue Goal

$-866,918

Backlog

Profit Variance

◇ T12M ◢◢ Goal

Profit Net Income %

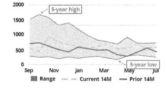

■ T12M Net Income % (Horizontal Bar)
— Prior T12M Net Income % (Vertical Bar)

TOTAL COMPANY

Revenue Goal

$6,814,130

Backlog

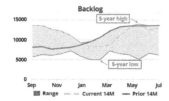

Profit Variance

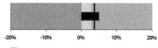

◇ T12M ◢◢ Goal

Profit Net Income %

■ T12M Net Income % (Horizontal Bar)
— Prior T12M Net Income % (Vertical Bar)

black horizontal bar is actual for current period. The vertical black bar represents the prior year percentage as a point of reference. You can see that it identifies valuable information at a glance about your progress toward realized profit as compared with prior year's profit. The ability to compare regions, products, even customers with all these data gives owners greater clarity, transparency, and accountability. You can answer the question of who is doing what toward the progress of the company in 10 seconds or less. How many thousands of man-hours are saved by automating your Profit Picture?

Color versions are available at profitpicture.net.

After the presentation, Sasha demonstrated the short-term benefits that Water Macro had already experienced by making the changes the employees had suggested and by allowing the employees to set their own hours each week. Although leaving the building open 24/7 tripled the electricity bill, the company recouped that cost with much higher productivity. Absences were down, productivity was up, and the product enhancing and marketing suggestions were flowing in.

"What's the next step?" Marlena asked.

"I would say that your next step is to subscribe to Profit Picture, to increase your use of the brainstorming harvest, and to step up Water Macro's presence on the national market. You need an expansion plan. As for the workplace, I think it would be a good idea, now that there's a cafeteria in place, to start looking for a way to bring in a preschool. Remember, these ventures cost you nothing and increase your productivity."

"Here are some questions," Sasha said, handing each woman a piece of paper. These questions were either inspired or directly created by Dan Sullivan, founder of The Strategic Coach® Program. You can take some time to answer these, and it will help you moving forward."

Questions for Business Owners

1. What is it worth to move quickly from a sense of confusion, isolation, and powerlessness to one of clarity, confidence, and capability?
2. What is your most important measurable?
3. What would expand your opportunity capacity?
4. What is the area that, if you made an improvement in it, would give you and others the greatest return on time, energy, and dollars invested?
5. What does progress mean to you?
6. What are you trying to make happen in the next three months?
7. What are you trying to make happen in the next 12 months?
8. What are you trying to make happen in the next three years?

9. What's the most important decision you're facing? What's keeping you from making it?
10. What area under your responsibility are you most satisfied with? Least satisfied with?
11. What part of your responsibilities are you avoiding right now?
12. What do you wish you had more time to do?

"You know," Jan said, reviewing the questions, "we may need you to manage this expansion."

Sasha's eyes widened and he asked, "Can you tell me more about what you are suggesting?"

"We would offer you a salaried position," Jan continued. "You would be traveling."

Sasha nodded. "I see. Thank you. Thank you both for considering me for this job. I am flattered and, at the same time, I have to turn it down. You see," he turned to the computer and opened up his own presentation, "I am busy developing a new product—a new business of my own. I would be very happy to help you find the right person for the expansion job, however."

Sasha waited. As traditional, hierarchical bosses, Jan and Marlena were not used to being turned down or to being told that their employees were starting their own companies.

Sasha spread his arms wide. "I know it may feel uncomfortable for you and awkward to move onto the playing field with me. Can we just sit with it for a minute? Even though we like to think that our control keeps our employees doing a good job, the truth is that they do the best job when we behave with kindness and respect. The rules are the rules. Your relationship with your employees can be deeper and wider than that of owner to machine or police to suspect. It can be co-creator, guide, co-learner, and supporter."

Marlena squinted up at the screen and nodded. "Point made, Sasha. What do you have going on?"

"This," Sasha said, "is called the WaterDrug Wall. Patents in the U.S., Canada, and EU pending." He handed them the hard copies and went through the presentation, explaining the market need in each segment.

Finally, he launched the page that showed what Water Macro would gain by being an umbrella for his company, "K'an 水."

"What is K'an? What does it mean? What does that symbol mean?" Jan asked.

"It means, 'danger' or 'water' in Chinese."

"Ohhhhh," they nodded but looked confused. "Why is water the same as danger?"

"Water represents telling the truth and also moving forward. Both of these are risky."

The room grew silent.

"This is a lot to absorb, Sasha," Marlena finally said. "I applaud you for your innovation. It's a great idea. It's not something we would ever do, I don't think, because we're not that public. Just to put your mind at ease. We don't want to get involved in the environmental side of things."

"Yes. That's true," Jan chimed in. "We have our lives to lead, and our interest is in running smoothly and increasing profits, but not too fast. We like to keep a low profile."

"Do I need to give you guys some time to consider this? I ran the numbers, and the fees and permits required for me to launch this product from a sterile, commercial location are more than I can handle and still develop the business."

"We're going to give it to our financial advisor," Marlena said as she gathered up the papers. "Your offer of four percent is fine. We just need to check on any liability issues and if we need to get a rider to the business insurance policy and how much that might cost."

"Also . . ." Jan noted, looking at Marlena, "we need to see if there is some sort of tax break for us if we support him."

Sasha nodded.

"We can let you know by next week. How does that sound?"

"Great."

They all shook hands, and Sasha passed on Victor's contact information so they could subscribe to the Profit Picture program. When it was all over, he went into the bathroom and took off his tie, folding it and putting it into his computer bag. He stared at his face in the mirror. Who was this Genghis Khan/

Hello Annie guy? He had one foot in this world and one foot in another. "Thank you," he whispered to God and Jesus Christ. "Thank you for Your presence that sustains me."

He walked out the door and to his station. He turned on the lights and began to measure the water.

He had made plans to have lunch with Suki on Sunday. So far, he had been too busy to visit her, but he realized he needed to make the time, just as he had needed to make the time with Julia, but hadn't. Suki lived in an old house in the foothills of the Klamath Mountains. She was house-sitting for a family that had gone to Africa for a year. Sasha drove out to her house and admired the view of snowcapped peaks as he walked up to the sprawling Arts and Crafts style home. Suki let him in and showed him around the charming rooms filled with pictures of the family and signs of a busy life.

"I keep this dusted and clean," she explained. "I actually live in the garage apartment. Sometimes I come in here just to read or play the piano because it feels nice." She took him to her apartment, where she'd made a delicious Korean lunch with many small dim sum dishes and chilies. The wafting fragrances filled Sasha's heart with longing for home. He slipped into the tiny kitchen and began tasting the ingredients in each pot. "Did you learn to cook Korean food when you were young, before you left Korea?"

"No. My American mom and I took lessons together. It's one way we bonded when I was adopted."

"That sounds like fun. Was it?"

Suki laughed, "No, ha, ha. No. It was a great experience and we both learned how to make Korean food, but it was *not* fun."

"What do you mean?"

"Well, I was so *angry* when I came to the United States. I acted badly. I sulked and talked back and was just in a lot of emotional pain. The cooking lessons were times when my adoptive mother and I argued and had fights with each other . . . a lot."

"Oh. Hmm. Why do you say it was a great experience?"

"Well, fighting was my way of engaging with someone without being vulnerable. I was too scared to be vulnerable. Once we argued and stuff, I began to feel safe with her. She stuck it out with me. When the cooking lessons were over, I let down my guard with her. So, it was all part of a process."

"What are your parents like?"

"Oh, they're nice. They're tall, blond missionaries with a lot of energy. They garden, work, bake, write books, travel. You name it, they do it. They're tolerant of different types of people but not different religions, which means they're not really tolerant of different types of people." She shrugged one shoulder. "They certainly gave me a lot of love. I can't complain." She laid the plates on the table. "Say, you just spent some time with your new dad. How was that?"

"Oh, it was good . . . super. We played chess. He showed me this cool software program he's using in his business. It's called Profit Picture. It's unusual because it integrates the company's data and then makes visual displays of assessments and predictions."

She nodded and said, "Nice. Did you go anywhere?"

"No. Well, we walked up the hill to the church. Hey," Sasha paused and looked at her quizzically, "hey, Suki, can I ask you something?"

She laughed and said, "I guess what you *mean* is, 'Can I ask you something *personal?*'"

"Yes," he said, nodding sheepishly.

"Sure. What do you want to know?"

"I was hoping that Victor and I could meditate together up on the hill. It's always much better when you do it with others, but Victor says that he doesn't meditate."

"And?"

"I was surprised. After all the reading I did, I just thought meditation was part of being a Christian. Jesus clearly tells his disciples to be still, to go into their closet, and somewhere there is another verse that discusses keeping your eye single and full of light. There are several references to meditation, you see. Suki, do you meditate?"

"Yes and no. I mean, I just started to since I met you. But listen, Sasha, why does it bother you? Isn't yoga meditation a practice that has no dogma? I was reading that dogma is considered a drag for yogis."

"Yes, that's true."

"Well, then, why would you want to expect anyone to do what you do? Besides," she continued, "the Christianity of the Orient is different from the Christianity of the Occident, the West: to each his own. Believe me, I was smack in the middle of people who thought their way was the only way. You don't want to be like that."

"You're right. I was attached to having an experience for myself. I wasn't thinking of him." Sasha paused.

"There's something else that came up," Sasha said.

"Talk away, but do it while we're eating." She had set the table and was putting the food out. Sasha sat down and poured them each a glass of water.

"Do you care if we talk about politics, kinda sorta?"

"No. I don't care. What is it?"

"Well, Victor was saying that basically, there are a lot of people here in the U.S. who are poor and they get government assistance. He's strongly opposed to this, saying that people need to work, not take handouts."

"Yes. You know that no one, including welfare recipients, would argue with that. I'm from Wisconsin. Do you know about how Wisconsin almost eliminated welfare?"

"No, what did they do?"

"They attached a work requirement to all benefits. There's a lot of job training and transitioning into the workforce. Most recipients loved it. They hated feeling, like, dependent, you know?"

"Cool." Sasha nodded. "Here in the United States, there is so much freedom. At the same time, there is so much conflict."

"And this bothers you?" Suki rapped his knuckles with her chopstick. "Sasha, didn't you ever have any conflict with your parents? I've told you about how I fought with my mom. Did you ever fight?" She sat back and looked at him, a curious expression in her emerald eyes.

Sasha shrugged. "You know, Suki, I did, but we didn't really argue. My mom had this . . . this script thing, and we used it whenever we were mad."

"What script thing?"

"Like, we would say whatever we observed the other person do that bothered us. Once I was mad at my mom for giving me an early curfew. So I said, 'I see that you set a rule that I have to come home by 11 PM.'"

"Yeah, or maybe like, 'I see that you ate all the icing off the cake in the fridge,'" Suki suggested.

"Right. So then, the person who is mad says how that particular action affected them. So I said, 'This early curfew makes it hard for me to go out with my friends and relax at a restaurant because then I only have one or two hours to be with them.'"

Suki smiled a slow, knowing smile. "Wait. Let me guess. Is the next thing you say a request for the other person to do something the way you want or need?"

Sasha nodded, "Yes. How did you know?"

"That's a system this guy, um, Marshall Rosenberg, invented. It's called Nonviolent Communication, or NVC. My mom is a social worker. She taught it to us too, but it was pretty late, after we'd already spent most of our time yelling and arguing in emotional outbursts."

"Oh." Sasha was quiet. He was surprised that his mom had been using a "system" all these years that wasn't her own invention.

He looked up and saw that Suki was watching him. "What?"

"Nothing. Look, Sasha, there's always going to be a lot of slinging and yelling when it comes to American politics. The right wants this, and the left wants that." She leaned back in her chair with a knowing expression. "There's a kind of secret weapon that you can use to cut through all the bull, if you want," she said.

"Yeah?" Sasha grinned. "What is it? I hope it's not an actual weapon."

"You know, I've lived in the slums of Korea, in an orphanage run by nuns, and in a northern, American state with a large group of evangelical fundamentalists I don't feel that comfortable with. What I got to learn from all of that is that love has nothing to do with being comfortable, being in agreement, or thinking the other person is fair. Love has no interest in the other person's wealth or their lack of it. It isn't concerned with their religion, their goodness, or even if they know who you are. *That* sword will slice right through just about anything."

Sasha looked at her, as if he were seeing her for the first time. Who was Suki? He stared at her and suddenly noticed that she was much smaller. Suki must have lost nearly 20 pounds since he'd last seen her, a month ago. Her face was less round, and her hair was a tower of tiny braids climbing an intricate trellis. This gave her height, and he had the sense that she was wearing a crown.

Suki stood up and said, "Leave the dishes for now. I want to show you my studio. We can have coffee and dessert in there." She opened the back door, motioning for him to follow without looking back.

They walked down the stairs and into the garage that used to be a carriage house under her apartment. As he walked through the sliding wooden doors, Sasha caught his breath. All around him, standing six feet tall each, were the most exquisite paintings he had ever seen. The barn-like space vibrated with intricate color and movement. He went instantly to the first painting and stood absorbed in it: A scene with a well and a large orange fish coming out of it, while out at sea, fishermen were casting nets. Children hung from tree branches playing with the fish.

He moved to the next and the next and the next. In all, there were eight paintings, each novel and completed with such skill that he felt flabbergasted with the beauty and the meaning of it all.

"No wonder you left medical school," he said, finally finding his voice.

Suki laughed happily, saying, "Thank you, that's reassuring. Hey, come sit down. Here's a plum cake and coffee."

Sasha walked in a daze over to the picnic table where she'd arranged a white cloth, cups, and a little cake. "This looks sort of . . . romantic," he said as he blinked.

"Don't worry, scaredy-cat. I'm not interested in you anymore."

"No?"

"No. You're too busy and caught up in all your business plans. I am really glad to get to see you now because we're friends, OK?"

Sasha nodded and smiled at her. "OK. You're right. I work two jobs, and I'm only free to see friends once a month or less. I didn't even call Julia back when she texted me, and you know how that turned out."

Suki made no reply. She was calm and feeling great. This was just the kind of lunch she had always dreamed of having: near the mountains with a good friend and good food. She just poured the coffee and they ate their cake in a companionable silence surrounded by art on the inside and mountains on the outside.

Driving home, Sasha had a funny feeling as if someone was flying a kite in his chest. It was somewhat disturbing.

Late the next day, he called Yusup.

"Ah, Sasha! My oldest son!" Yusup sounded jolly. "You calling me with women problems?"

Sasha laughed, slightly embarrassed. "No. No women problems." He could hear children in the background. Suddenly, a loud noise came over the phone and he nearly dropped it. "What was that?!"

"Oh, that was just Emily. She is yelling for her bottle."

"Who is Emily?" Even as he asked the question, he knew the answer. Emily was vocal.

"My daughter!" Yusup cooed like a proud papa. "We moved. We live in a big house now, way up north. Yu Hong is a lawyer . . . immigration! She work all the time. I take care of the house and children. I am a house-husband!"

Sasha couldn't believe what he was hearing. It was surprising to imagine Yusup switching roles, to be sure, but more surprising was his manner. He was so exuberant and happy. The whole time growing up, Sasha had felt the pall of their flight from China hanging over Yusup. He laughed and joked, but always in a controlled way. Usually, he stayed in the little back yard, studying science journals or experimenting with a small vegetable garden.

Yusup was barely audible since he had the phone on speaker and was changing the baby's diaper.

"When you come to visit, you can swim in the pool!"

"Yusup, you sound like you're doing well. I can't wait to meet my little sister."

"Yes! You come!"

They said goodbye, and Sasha hung up the phone, pulling into his driveway with five minutes to spare before his shift with Al started.

As he relieved the day nurse and took up his post with Al, he tried to put what Suki said about him being too busy to have a relationship out of his mind. He'd made a plan, he was sticking to it. Wasn't that a good thing? Women.

Chapter 9

You Can't Legislate Morality

Experience should teach us to be most on our guard to protect liberty when the Government's purposes are beneficent. Men born to freedom are naturally alert to repel invasion of their liberty by evil-minded rulers. The greatest dangers to liberty lurk in the insidious encroachment by men of zeal, well meaning but without understanding.

—Louis D. Brandeis

Sasha opened the locked safe in his home lab. Inside were antidepressants of every kind: Prozac, Zoloft, Paxil, Luvox, Lexapro, Celexa, Vilazodone. He had been able to purchase them online. They were shipped from Singapore, and the company had its own doctor sign the prescriptions. He also had in the fridge diet sodas, concentrations of caffeine, pain medications, and heart medications, and, of course, Cialis. For each of these ingredients, he had the standard trace test to find out the concentration of the ingredient in a water sample. He had to alter and refine some of the basic tests, such as the test for diet soda. Studies showed that people who took antidepressants over long periods of time, also consumed vast amounts of diet soda. Sasha had considered testing for marijuana and cocaine, too, but decided against it. These substances weren't showing up in the water in large amounts, according to the published research he'd read.

Once he had the basic tests in hand and knew the most commonly found levels of each across the U.S., he set about to devise tests that took no longer than one hour to show results. His experiments in this area had progressed rapidly, and he was now devising a neon billboard that could effectively broadcast the test results twice a day with only minimal human monitoring, if any. This proved to be an electrical-chemical challenge that he enjoyed. "I'm not just a lab guy, I'm a light engineer!" He'd relished the foray into digital translation of chemical codes into neon numbers. "It has to be big enough to be readable from a highway going about 40 mph," he told the digital-sign builders.

In less than three months, his WaterPurity Data test was set to ship to beta testers in his own city of Richmond and in nearby Sacramento.

"Yes, things are moving along," Sasha thought to himself. He had filed the legal papers for his corporation, *K'an*. He was effectively working 20 hours a week for himself and 35 for Water Macro. Although he had very little free time, he was still carefully cultivating his friendships with both Julia and Suki. Naturally, he stayed in touch with Victor. These days, they texted, emailed, and, every once in a while, sent a letter. Victor had promised that they would take a trip together at Christmas. He said it would be a surprise.

Sasha had defined each phase of market expansion: First, he would market to water purifiers and bottled-water companies. After that, he didn't know how long exactly, probably 18 months, he would market to municipalities in dense urban areas. Finally, he would refine fast tests for nitrates, insecticides, herbicides, and fecal matter and market the tests to rural areas in the U.S. and in developing nations.

In fact, Sasha was holding onto some thrilling news that he had not shared yet with anyone. European Union representatives had already contacted him, indicating a strong interest in making a purchase as soon as possible.

The states of New Jersey, Kansas, and Missouri had also reached out. It seemed they were in intense competition with their neighboring states for businesses to locate within their borders. They needed the tax revenues, in some cases. In others, they needed to maintain a reputation as having a healthy environment for families. Sasha was hoping to gain momentum with Kentucky and Florida, two states with high drug use concentrated in specific areas.

Vancouver and Toronto had sent him letters of interest, and he told them the test would be available to the Canadian market in about six months.

How did all these places come to learn of the WaterPurity Data? His patents had alerted some of them. The website he put up had helped, and a scientific article he'd submitted to the *Journal of the American Chemical Society* had been published. Sasha realized as he fell asleep involuntarily and began to forget things, that he was exhausted. He'd pushed himself for so long that he had no idea what real rest felt like any more. Yes, he took time to meditate, and he slept about five hours each night. Still, the constant pressure of working three jobs and maintaining the legal and marketing connections for the new business was taking its toll. Until he could produce income with the WaterPurity Data, he could not afford to stop working at Water Macro.

He realized that he really needed to stop working at Water Macro. He needed a small business loan, but he was loath to borrow. He considered living off his savings, but he knew that they were so depleted already that it was not wise. His idea of selling purified water as a byproduct of his testing had gone in the trash once he realized how many additional licenses he needed to manufacture a consumable product on top of those required just to run a commercial lab. There was no way he could pay the legal, health department, city, state, and federal fees.

What to do? Sasha racked his brain to think of a way to put an extra $10,000 in his pocket. He knew that many business owners might consider this small change, but it wasn't. It was the difference between making it and dying trying. This, he realized, was why rich people made it and poorer people with great ideas did not. Family money that gives you a cushion makes the difference in many cases. He knew that he could ask Victor for a loan, but he also knew that Victor would make the offer on his own if that's what he wanted to do.

Finally, he decided to borrow the money. He wanted a 12-month delay in repayment, however, and he knew that the SBA would want him to begin repaying any monies they loaned immediately—ridiculous but true. He got online and found a competitive lending website where he could set the terms of the loan and various banks could compete for his business. It took him a while, but he finally found a lender. The interest rate was 5 percent, up one point for the deferred repayment, but he felt this was a good deal, nevertheless.

With the check in the bank, Sasha tendered his resignation at Water Macro. Jan and Marlena were reluctant to let him leave, especially since he'd be staying in their building, just down the hall. "How about coming in and doing a training once in a while for new brainstorming leaders?" Marlena asked. "We can pay you well."

Sasha smiled, "Tempting! The truth is, Marlena, the more that you and Jan can work with your team, the more trust you can develop with them and the greater your return on your investment in them. Let them see you honestly participating in brainstorming along with them. Let them see you take down their ideas with acceptance and, most of all, let them see you follow, laugh, and generally be vulnerable. This will affect the culture of your company more than anything else. And," he added, " . . . the culture of your company is your weakest point."

Jan gulped and said, "I guess it's time for me to stop hiding behind my desk and my office door."

"Me too," Marlena looked guilty. "We need to get out there and walk our talk, or we're just going to have one half-baked revamp."

So, Sasha shook their hands and said goodbye. In the new cafeteria, the employees laid out a homemade feast they brought from home: spicy finger foods from every Asian country weighed the table down. In the middle was the great delicacy of spicy chicken feet. Sasha made a point of going back and getting three helpings of every dish. His forehead was sweating and his stomach bloated, but he wanted to demonstrate his love for these people. Shoving rice balls into his mouth was the least he could do.

Even though he never saw any of his co-workers outside the lab, he felt that they were part of his family. He promised to stop by and, when he left the building, to have them all over for a grand opening wherever he landed.

That Saturday, Suki suggested that instead of going downtown to the park, they go to the beach. It was still summer, and the surfers dotted the sea while children lingered in the sand. He agreed to meet her at China Beach at 10 in the morning. When he got to the shore, a mist hung over the flowering bushes on the bluffs. He could barely see the arch of the Golden Gate Bridge in the distance, and the water was choppy. His phone rang. It was Suki.

"Sasha, are you already at the beach?"

"Yes."

"I have some bad news. . . . My father has passed away."

"Oh! I'm so sorry!"

"He was 90 years old, Sasha. He lived a full life, and he died in his sleep. I've got to fly up to Minnesota right now. I'm sorry to miss our monthly time together."

"Oh. Yes. Don't worry about it. Is there anything I can do to help you?"

"No. I've got a neighbor watching the house for me while I'm gone. I'll be back in three days, in time for your dinner party."

"How is it with your soul?"

"Yes. I'm sad. He was a good dad. I never knew my Korean dad, so he was my only one. He was a good man, Sasha. He was gentle and quiet. He taught kids after he retired, and they all loved him."

"You call me if you need to talk."

"I will. I will. It may be rough for me."

"I'm here. Call or email me."

They said goodbye, and Sasha sat down on the sand, thinking of Suki. He was a supergeek, he knew that. He'd actually never kissed a girl or really had a girlfriend. None of the guys in the Numbers group had, back when they were all hanging out together. He missed those guys. Another man in the group had sent out an SOS request two weeks ago for data about a kind of sonic device and the history of an obscure trucking company in Iran. Sasha had helped him just as he had been helped. The hacking was important *and* he could see how the risk of being in touch was too high. Still, he missed them. Forcing data access for the sake of citizen safety and information was dangerous. It was no game. They could not take any additional risks.

He slowly lay down in a cool sand trough and closed his eyes. How long he slept, he didn't know, but he woke to the sound of the Uyghur alphabet song somewhere above him. A dream . . . .

Sasha opened his eyes and saw the sky, like a fluttering piece of gray linen, and then the solid outline of a body sitting next to him. He rolled over away from the other person and sat up facing them: A small woman wearing a scarf over her head. Sasha crawled on all fours toward the figure. She turned to face him.

"Mother!" he cried out one time in a cracked voice half-audible from shock.

"Sasha," she said, smiling at him and reaching out her hand to touch his cheek. Then, he was crushing her in his embrace, crying.

"Mother, Mother, Mother . . . . Why did you leave me?"

She held him and let him cry. Finally, he pulled away. So much emotion was unusual for Sasha. Where did that come from? He looked down, afraid that the waves of relief and pain could not be controlled. What if he could not stop crying? With a mighty effort, he held himself together and feigned a calmness he did not feel.

They spoke in Uyghur, slowly forming sentences. She began, "A good mother lets her children fail and discover their own way. I knew I must leave you."

"Where *were* you?"

"I went back to my village in the Himalayas. I missed it after so many years. Babama died there while I was away. I lived in the little house where I grew up with Babama. I taught the children and spent time with my friends in the little town. I had to do some more work too. You see, I had left some money in a bank in Turkey. . . . Getting it out was complicated."

"Victor told me you were worried about me when I was in London."

"Yes." She ran her fingers through his red curls. "Your hair is so funny and wonderful." She giggled and then laughed freely and loudly. She had carried many secrets for such a long time, it was good to let them swim away in the present moment. She became more serious and said, "Victor tells me you are stepping out into the world of business?"

Sasha nodded. He stood up and put out his hands to her. "Let's walk." She let him pull her up, and he was surprised at how light she was. This was not polite, but he said it anyway, "Mother, you are sixty years old now." She narrowed her left eye and then smiled enigmatically and said, "Maybe."

They walked along the water without speaking. The sun had come out, and Sasha could see the bridge clearly in the distance. He reached down and took his mother's hand. "You will not leave me again."

"No. I won't," she said and paused. "But Sasha, I don't live here. I have a house down south, in Southern California. You and Victor are coming for Christmas, I think."

"Where is it?"

"It is in the Colorado Desert in a little town called Borrego Springs. There are beautiful flowers during the springtime. It is quiet. I see lizards and roadrunners sometimes. They are running out of water, son." She squeezed his hand.

"Mommy," he spoke the English word playfully, "I don't drill wells, I only test water."

"I know," she nodded. He had a feeling that she had something up her sleeve, but he knew he would have to wait.

"When you come to see me, we will see the stars at night. They are very beautiful in the desert."

After walking to the cliffs, they turned around and walked back. He took her to her car. "Can you come have lunch with me? We can go to Chinatown together." She nodded happily, and he could see that Nur had long been waiting for the joys of friendship with her son. She had worked so hard to be his mother.

They decided to take the train all the way into the city. As it sped along, Nur told him many things. She talked of her life with Sasha and Yusup and how much she relished the safety of living away from the Chinese government. Sasha studied her face for signs of hatred. Victor had told him that after her arrest, she had been tortured before being assigned to counter-intelligence. There was no hatred in those black eyes, only peace, unruffled peace. He realized that the conjectures of his younger self that his parents missed being told what to do by the government were far from true. Clearly, they had both despised the Communists who had enslaved Nur and tried to have all of them slaughtered during the ethnic cleansing.

He told her how Yusup was caring for young children in a fancy house with a young lawyer wife. She smiled, quite pleased. "He has found balance. In balance is happiness."

His mother's smooth face revealed age only when she leaned her face against the window. Her eyes were less open, the lids falling over them as if she were trying to remember something. Her shoulders remained square and pointed—arrows ready to fire—and her hands, able to toss an assassin over her back or toss a poisoned dart, were folded origami swans in her lap. As always, her hair framed her face in a smooth black cap, pulled back and twisted against her neck. Julia sometimes wore her hair like that too. He had asked Julia once, "What do you call this way of twisting your hair at the neck? You and my mother are the only women I have ever seen wear your hair this way."

"Chignon."

Julia was coming to see him the day after tomorrow. She was stopping by on her way to Japan. He'd asked Rose for the night off and arranged a little dinner on the second floor of the house for Julia. Suki, Victor, and Al and Al's daytime caregiver were all going to be there. Sasha had cleaned the house and carefully made enchiladas, which were Julia's favorite food. He froze them uncooked, according to Suki's instructions.

"Mother! You must come stay with me for a couple of days. I'm having a dinner party for my friends, and Victor is coming. Won't you come?" He looked at her pleadingly.

She nodded. "Yes, of course. I am here now, and I can spend time with you without any problem. That would be lovely, to meet your friends and see Victor."

"Have you not seen him?" She shook her head.

"No. We've had long discussions over the phone."

"Mother, I have some big news, and you will be the first to know."

She looked at him expectantly, saying nothing.

"The EU and two American cities and two Canadian cities have contacted me, expressing an interest in purchasing the WaterPurity Data test once it is through beta testing."

"How exciting!" Nur hugged him and did a little happy dance in her seat. Her face shone with pride. "Ah, every Chinese mother's dream," she joked in Mandarin, "a son who is successful."

They laughed lightly together, understanding the joke. Nur's definition of success did not necessarily include business or wealth.

After their outing in San Francisco, Sasha and his mother drove from the Richmond train station to the palatial house where he lived. When she walked through the front doors, she stood quietly in the center of the living room. "It is a stage."

She looked at him and said, "Your stage."

He nodded and moved down the hallway. She came behind him, and he showed her the room where she could stay. It was the master bedroom with one wall of windows looking down over the hillside and out to sea in the far distance. He pointed out to her the knoll where deer sometimes gathered at dusk and early morning.

She sat on the giant king-sized bed that looked like a grape on a leaf. He smiled. "Will you be OK? I have to go relieve the day nurse. Come over to the kitchen area after about an hour. I want you to meet Al once he's had his dinner and stuff."

She nodded, casually looking over the room with her spy's eye for possible dangers and additional escape routes. He noticed this.

Would she ever change? Would she always live one step away from the grip of an unknown evil? Sasha shook his head as he closed her door and walked toward the kitchen. "I bet I'm the only kid in the world who has two Cold War-era spies from two different countries for parents," he thought. "I'm like Harry Potter with espionage heritage instead of magic."

While he served Al his rice and mung beans, Sasha said, "Hey, Al, my mom is here. She came to visit me."

Al's eyes lit up from his usual dull stare. "Where is she?"

"She's in the master bedroom. She's going to come in and say hi to you once you're in your pajamas and we've done the oxygen treatment."

Al nodded. He perked up noticeably at the prospect of a female visitor.

Once he had had his teeth brushed, taken his meds, been lifted into bed, and lay with the oxygen mask over his face for eight minutes, Sasha rang the bell by the side of the bed.

On cue, Nur quietly entered the room and slipped up to the side of the bed, laying her hand on the railing. She spoke to Al softly in Mandarin, bowing slightly, saying, "It is a great pleasure to meet you, Sir."

Al's face transformed into a soft smile. "The honor is all mine," he answered. "What is your name?"

"My name is Bo Nur. I come from the western part of China. You are from Singapore?"

And so they began to chat and share with one another. Sasha quietly moved to the back of the room to a grouping of couches and lamps where he usually spent time meditating or researching when he was not sleeping on his bed at the foot of Al's.

He picked up a book of poetry, *Spring Essence*, by Ho Xuan Huong, ancient Vietnamese poems recovered from an oral language by the translator John Balaban. Ah, a rare treat. Sasha immersed himself in the poems. When the time grew near for him to take Al to the bathroom, he glanced up. Al was talking, talking, long and distinctly without stopping, to Nur. She stood by his side, holding his hand, listening intently. He was telling her his life story, everything that had ever happened to him. He spoke with the voice and intonations he'd once had as a younger man. Sasha saw that he had come to the end, summing up the loves and losses and sorrows in his life. He clutched Nur's hand and asked her a question insistently, half rising from the bed.

She calmly answered without emotion and lightly patted his chest.

He lay back down and smiled wanly, coughed a few times, and then he was gone.

Sasha froze under the lamp, unable to move. What had just happened?

Nur gently laid Al's hand by his side and covered his face with the blanket. She turned to Sasha and said, "He has left his body. Please call his daughter. You and I must clean his body and dress him in his everyday clothes. It is Buddhist tradition."

Sasha walked into the next room and called Rose, then he got out Al's soft brown corduroy pants, a white shirt, and walking shoes. They quietly prepared the body and laid it on top of the covers, keeping their thoughts peaceful and prayerful.

"Now I will sing," said Nur. She put her hand on the forehead of the dead man for a moment and began to sing a chant that encouraged the soul to travel on with peace and the love of those it leaves behind.

The rest of the evening was a string of strangely quiet events. Rose and her husband came and prayed and chanted until daylight. Then, the funeral parlor sent a car to retrieve the body.

Because he had to work the next day, Sasha retired to a bedroom on the first floor and slept. In the morning, he found Rose and his mother drinking tea in the kitchen. He said good morning and joined them at the table.

"Rose, I only have a few minutes before I have to leave for work. I would like to talk to you and your husband about purchasing this house from you when you are free later today or this week."

"Sasha, you know it is not . . . it has no value except for its materials at this point. Even then, it would be difficult to transport or remove them without great expense."

He nodded. "Yes, I know. I need a gathering place, and, even though it may be swallowed up by the earth at any moment, I am willing to take that risk."

"Why do you need a gathering place?" Rose asked.

"I'm forming a new kind of citizen brainstorming group. We're going to meet and develop free-market solutions to social and economic problems to limit the reach of government. It's a group that won't be associated with any political party. I'm hoping that the energy will grow and spread and that it have a positive influence on the country as a whole."

Rose looked at him stoically and then glanced at his mother. "You have an unusual son."

Nur nodded and said, "He is full of enthusiasm." She used the Chinese word for "enthusiasm," *Yü* , which means persuasive and able to gather many helpers together in support of a new idea.

Rose put down her cup. "We can talk tomorrow evening after the funeral. I will sell you this house for one dollar."

Sasha then did something that was not Chinese but American: He put out his hand and Rose took it. They shook hands like two Texans over a fence, then they bowed to one another, and he said, "I am so sorry for the loss of your father. I loved Al. He was a sweet man."

"Thank you." Rose, who always looked tired, let a tear form in her eye. She turned away. Sasha left the two women together and sprinted out the front door for the bus. Yes, it was Sunday, but he had to complete and submit an experiment for peer review and possibly publishing. He also needed to review construction of the 30-foot-wide WaterPurity Data board in a phone meeting with the builders. Later on in the week, he would be driving to the warehouse in Sacramento and watching one of the first live tests of the board.

Life was moving fast for Sasha. Getting the citizen's brainstorming coalition off the ground would take more than just ideas. He needed *something else* that would draw people in so that a wider range of people would come and participate instead of just intellectuals and political activists. He needed art and music and . . . fun. He remembered a word, *lagniappe*, a Cajun word maybe? It meant something extra added for spice, he thought. Perhaps . . . perhaps . . . six or seven eight-foot-tall paintings would attract a crowd. He would ask Suki. Perhaps, also, some stunning classical or folk music . . . .

Julia was due to come in tonight. Suki would be returning to Sasha's tomorrow morning. He had planned the dinner party at the same time that Al's funeral would be occurring. He would have to have it right after the funeral. Whew. So many details! His head swam with the data rushing around in it. On top of everything, HIS MOTHER HAD COME BACK!

He reached Water Macro and made his way to his lab space in the rear of the building. The whole world was aglow with the light of his happiness. His family was here, and everything was OK.

That evening, Julia, Nur, and Sasha went for a walk after dinner. They came to the top of the hill where the abandoned church rose up, its white and gold dome shimmering in the deepening darkness. When they reached the church, they separated, each walking in a different direction to investigate or wander. Julia's arrival had been joyous, and Sasha was pleased to find her relaxed and much more outgoing. Her ordeal had transformed her from a quiet, dutiful daughter, to an adult in her own right. She was beautiful, as always, but her beauty was now eclipsed by her new way of being witty and a little bit "take charge."

She had accepted a position with the Japanese government as a leader in a new push to develop healthy lifestyles in Japan. Apparently, the Japanese culture was dying. Japanese people worked such long hours that the birthrate had fallen to double negative digits. Many young men died each year from work-related stress and heart attacks. It was common for a Japanese child to have only met his or her father a few times. Something had to be done to change the downward spiral of this country. The government had specifically sought out young people of Japanese descent born in the United States, thinking that they would be able to bring both an appreciation of Japanese culture and the ability to introduce more leisure time and family time into the average Japanese lifestyle. They wanted new ideas, and Julia had them. Julia was excited also, he could tell, to get away from the home nest and become more independent.

Whenever she was in the company of another person, his mother was able to bring out the pearl hidden in them. She asked questions and listened with real delight to what they had to say, until a subtle glow came over them. Watching her with Julia, Sasha wondered if he had ever seen anyone listen to her in the same way. Did she ever wish for that? Like many grown children, he vaguely realized that his mother was a separate person apart from her role as his mother, but the idea only touched his mind briefly.

Half an hour later, the three came back together and walked home singing old jazz tunes, "The Way You Look Tonight" and "Fly Me to The Moon."

Julia was staying across the hall from Nur. Sasha had to get a room ready for Victor, who would arrive in the morning. Just in case, he also prepared a room for Suki, who was arriving a few hours after Victor.

The next day, Julia and Nur went out and bought flowers that they spent some time arranging for the table. His mother made little pots of mango pudding for dessert. She was just pouring the pudding into the pots when the doorbell rang.

Sasha opened the front door to find Victor bearing a large white box before him. "I brought a few gifts." Victor was dressed all in white, including his shoes and a white fedora. "I got your message about how to dress for a Buddhist funeral. I hope this is OK."

He put his boxes down and grabbed Sasha's hand. "Is she here?" Victor asked. Sasha nodded toward the kitchen. He could feel Victor's pulse pounding. Stepping lightly across the yellow carpet, Victor walked into the kitchen. Nur looked up and saw a tall man whose curly white ringlets mingled with his suit in a most extraordinary way. Her eyes widened with the shock of how he had changed after so long, then she looked down, suddenly shy.

Sasha went to find Julia and left his parents to themselves.

Julia was dressed for the funeral and working on her computer. "I'm just going to change," he told her. She glanced at him. "Come sit down and talk to me. How are you doing with so many corns popping?"

"Fine. Exhausted. Strange. Freaked out." He grinned. "I'm cool."

"Thank you for helping me this year, Sasha. I'm here because of you."

"Julia, you're here, my mom and Victor are here. Suki is coming. It's going to be great to have almost everyone close to me in the same room."

"Who is missing?"

"Yusup. Yusup is missing. He is still my father too." She nodded and said, "Your mom and I will be the only people there who knew you when you had black hair." They chatted on casually, and Sasha felt at ease with Julia. He could tell that she no longer harbored feelings for him.

He left her and had just finished dressing, when his mother knocked on his door, "Your other friend, Suki, is here, Sasha."

There she stood, coming from the funeral of her father to Al's funeral. He held her in a long hug, her eyes were sad, and she gave him a small smile. "Are you going to introduce me to everyone?"

When Nur met Suki, she held her hand and said, "Hello Suki. So pleased to meet my new friend."

When Julia met Suki, she spoke to her in Korean and the two young women quickly formed a bond in the car on the way to the funeral.

Victor shook Suki's hand and said, "I finally get to meet you, Suki. I have heard from Sasha that you are a gifted painter. I wonder if you are showing your work in Portland?"

Suki laughed as if he had told a wonderful joke. "I will be showing in Portland soon. As soon as I find a gallery."

"Let's huddle later," he winked at her. Then, everyone quickly bundled into cars and zipped into the city to a small room on the grounds of the Botanical Garden that had a glass roof and a giant bonsai tree growing out of the floor.

Al's funeral was simple. The priest sang a traditional prayer song and spoke of how death folded into life as naturally as a leaf folds into the earth. Suki wiped her eyes.

Once back at the house, everyone sat down to the carefully prepared enchilada feast.

Sasha wanted to keep the conversation inclusive around the table, so that people did not just talk to one another the whole evening. He had always loved the feeling of being with a group of friends, and he'd been haunted recently by the loss of contact with his friends in the Numbers group.

Over mango pudding and fragrant tea, he asked, "So, have you heard of the Securing Individualism and Freedom Together Coalition Victor and I are starting here at the house?"

"I've heard about it," Suki said, "but I'm not sure exactly why. I mean, what is it you're trying to solve or do?"

"Isn't it," Julia asked, "about the people solving problems instead of the government?"

"Well, I don't really see that," Suki said.

"What do you mean?" Victor asked her. "What part of it?"

"The part where the people solve the problems. Let's face it, there are thousands of problems facing us right now that are pretty simple to solve, but the people don't do anything until they are forced to by the government. For example," she said, "here in California, they passed a law that stores can't hand out plastic bags. This is because there is an island of plastic, much of it grocery bags, the size of Texas floating in the ocean. When the plastic degrades into the sea, we end up having petrochemicals migrate into our bodies, soil, and food.

This has been going on for a long time. So, in the city of San Francisco, they can't give you a bag, but in neighboring cities, the same large chains give out bags. They could, of their own accord, stop handing out plastic bags, but they don't. They wait until forced to do so by the government, even though it harms us all."

"I think what you are talking about is morality," Victor said. "We all know the old saying, 'You can't legislate morality.'"

"You *can* legislate morality," Sasha said, "but when you do, you degrade both capitalism and democracy." He turned to Suki and said, "The grocery store chain is making a decision to give away their freedom rather than voluntarily spend money on a change."

"I know that over-legislation degrades capitalism, but does it degrade democracy just because it makes the government bigger?" Julia asked.

"Yes, well, it makes the government bigger, and we know from history that the nature of government is to infringe on the rights of the people," Victor said. "So, the answer is yes, the bigger the government, the greater the infringement and the risk of losing civil freedoms."

At this, a brief silence fell over the small group.

"This group, this coalition, will be a kind of stick that stirs the pot, won't it?" Nur asked. "Won't you be taking something that citizens do or should be doing all the time, coming up with solutions and talking about them, and rebranding it as something new and exciting and powerful?"

Sasha and Victor both blinked at the same time. "Rebranding?" Sasha said. "Huh. I see what you mean. It's not really new, it's just lain unused for so long."

"What has?" asked Suki, "Participation? Imagination?"

"We have some participation," Victor answered her, "but it is incredibly low and partisan. What we want to do is, as Nur said, stir the pot until the sense of ownership and even the belief that we can make a difference bubbles up and over into the greater culture, changing the very fabric of politics, and, yes, I do think that eventually, the business owners who are now raping the earth and robbing the people because they can, that even they will change on their own because that is the strength of culture."

"I'm not trying to be argumentative," Suki pressed, "but you said that the issue at the root of things is morality, right? Just the same thing that Confucius said. You're saying that people will be stimulated by the act of brainstorming, implementing solutions, and being with the group—group mentality. OK, but what about the problems that have always been with us?"

"You mean poverty," said Victor.

"Yes. The solution to poverty has many layers. One layer is to encourage self-reliance and self-development."

"Isn't that the only solution, really?" asked Julia.

Suki leaned forward to look at Julia and said, "No. No, it's not. Before you can motivate or engage someone, you have to meet them where they are and address their survival need at that moment. We can't say we've solved poverty simply by motivating people and providing opportunity for personal growth."

"Are you perhaps thinking of these verses from the Bible?" Victor asked. He closed his eyes and recited:

"For I was hungry and you gave me something to eat, I was thirsty and you gave me something to drink, I was a stranger and you invited me in, I needed clothes and you clothed me, I was sick and you looked after me, I was in prison and you came to visit me.'

"Then the righteous will answer him, 'Lord, when did we see you hungry and feed you, or thirsty and give you something to drink? When did we see you a stranger and invite you in, or needing clothes and clothe you? When did we see you sick or in prison and go to visit you?'

"The King will reply, 'Truly I tell you, whatever you did for one of the least of these brothers and sisters of mine, you did for me.'"

Sasha cleared his throat and said, "We have to first have compassion for the helpless and then give them the tools to become self-reliant."

"I believe that we are doing that in the United States to some extent," Victor pointed out. "For example, I am a member of a group of people in Portland who go each month to an area of the city that is suffering from lack of jobs and opportunity. We provide a dinner for parolees and their families. We also invite the parole officers so the parolees can meet with them without having to transfer across town if they don't have access to a car. Finally, we give them job counseling and opportunities to work in internships and apprenticeships, or even to enroll in job training such as nurse's aide or plumber or auto mechanic."

"Wow, that's pretty cool," Suki acknowledged. "It is true that if more people reached out with their hands and their hearts, that human kindness would propel people out of poverty. I'm saying that it's not the food or the opportunity or the money that propels people out of poverty, it's the evidence of good will and kindness that gives them the sense of being valued and the desire to move toward a more hopeful life of *inclusion in the group*. The *stuff* helps, of course, but we could easily eradicate poverty if more people just cared. That's why I think it is a good idea to stir the pot with this coalition stick, Sasha. Maybe you can light a firecracker under us all."

Sasha said, "Oh, that's similar to what I've been telling the owners at Water Macro. I told them that they cannot just put in a cafeteria, offer daycare, and set up brainstorming groups. They actually have to communicate love and kindness as one person to another. Otherwise, their business will only grow for a little while, then it will shrink again."

"Narcissism," Nur murmured.

"What?" Suki said. "*What* did you say?"

"Narcissism: the failure to recognize other people apart from one's own identity. What I hear Sasha saying is that to be successful in running a business or in eradicating poverty, you have to be unceasingly vulnerable and humble and continuously imagine how the other person feels. When they sense that level of humanity, they often rise to their highest selves. Love inspires morality."

The table fell quiet again as all eyes rested on the small woman who had three empty pudding pots in front of her.

Victor laughed a deep, resonating laugh. "Oh, how I sometimes wish I could have spent the last twenty years sharing a table with you!"

Gentle laughter sprinkled throughout the group as people gradually began to talk to the person sitting next to them. Slowly, the group relaxed into itself, and then the party was over.

Sasha stood up and began to clear the table. He said to Julia and Suki, "Come on, you guys, help me do the dishes." Julia and Suki began picking up plates, and they all three retired to the kitchen while Nur and Victor remained at the table sipping their tea.

Chapter 10

Everything Is a Gift

True freedom is impossible without a mind made free by discipline.
—Mortimer J. Adler

Three years later . . . .

He laid his glasses on the nightstand and lifted his legs onto the bed. As his head settled onto the pillow, Sasha pressed the remote control and the overhead light went out, leaving him in the darkened room. Across the ceiling passed the shadows from the moonlit clouds.

Ah, the anticipation of rest, what could be more wonderful? He smiled. The moments he had just spent during meditation exchanging words of love with his divine Friend and Master had been even more wonderful than the eclipse of sleep.

The day and the months that lay behind him felt like a dream. He knew that his mother would assure him, if she were sitting there in the room with him, that they were a dream, that all earthly reality was a dream.

Two days ago, he had returned from his mother's house in the desert. . . .

Needing a break from the press of his growing company, Sasha had taken a long weekend and grabbed the train that ran from San Francisco all the way down to San Diego. He'd rented a car and driven out through the vast, winding mountains that enclosed the Anza-Borrego desert. As he rounded the high bend and caught sight of the small village below, his heart lifted. Soon he would be on the little adobe patio watching the sun set in silence with Nur.

His mother had been living quietly in her little desert casita now for three years. She taught Qi Gong and hydroponic gardening to the locals and tourists. Every once in a while and for holidays, Sasha and Victor—or both— came to stay.

Three years ago, when his business had fully launched, Sasha traveled the world extensively to form alliances with nations and companies everywhere, from Disney World to Oman. As soon as the initial round of contracts had been signed, he passed the travel duties on to a rotating group of representatives. He remembered the issues about travel: that one did not get paid for the entire time away and that the costs to one's body and personal life were far greater than any amount of money. He had enjoyed spending a week with Yusup and Yu Hong and their two children, Jimmy and Emily. They sat by the pool laughing and talking and playing with the children. His long, agonizing walk away from his father that fateful day at the airport had finally ceased to torture him. Sasha had relaxed into the moment when Yusup's perpetually smiling face had shown him how wonderful that could be.

Sasha's organization had blossomed and spurted and climbed like a wild vine up through the world of commerce. His main focus had quickly become communicating and establishing the kind of workforce he wanted to have. He had specifically chosen the "Teal Level" model for his company, using the terminology from the book *Reinventing Organizations*. He believed in a flat hierarchy that would outlast him or any other personality.

Hours and hours of his time were invested in training and teaching both how to brainstorm and how to use the ideas that came from brainstorming. He spent many more hours facilitating tiered levels of groups that worked together to make decisions throughout the company. No one person or small group of people was responsible for anything at WaterPurity Data. His marketing and sales people were continuously informed by and informing the manufacturing, customer service, financial, and human resource people. In fact, so many of the employees at WaterPurity Data had cross skills and expertise that they often moved from one part of the organization to another. He was happy to see cross-fertilization of all kinds because he knew that it not only enhanced his product and sales but also the sense that the employees had of being valuable and listened to. The more they believed that what they had to say was taken seriously, the more golden nuggets they shared.

As soon as he could, he implemented the Profit Picture application, which validated the application's tagline, "Actionable Information." Every month, he made a series of Profit Picture graphs available to every employee. If there were problems or possible problems, he noted these and asked everyone to consider solutions.

Having visuals of the internal processes proved to be invaluable in such a wide open forum. These graphs and diagrams not only gave everyone a handle on the big picture, they also educated employees on how their actions and ideas worked or didn't work. The result was consistent cash flow, along with documentation about what factors contributed to that result.

Sasha had come to appreciate any form of criticism or complaint from one of his employees. He could pay consultants to come in and give him estimates on how operations were going . . . or he could honestly listen to and question the people who worked in the business day to day. If they trusted him, they would tell him the truth.

This sort of open dialogue included his customers, who had become accustomed to calling and discussing any and all ideas, problems, and business issues. Sasha listened to their business issues because he knew that someday, he might be able to help them solve one of their problems; if he could be of assistance either with information or with something more tangible, he would be.

One day, he had taken a call from a hotel chain in the United Arab Emirates. The next day, he had spoken to the woman who owned a fleet of fishing vessels in Alaska. For Sasha, profit came in many forms: money, brand recognition, new and imaginative ideas, ways to fit into his customer's lifestyle by meeting their business desires and solving their business problems, low turnover, repeat business, trust, and pervasive goodwill. The global marketplace had expanded the idea of profit considerably. Sasha was indeed gathering together all these forms of profit, keeping in mind that tomorrow it could all change. After all, the WaterPurity Data test was a technological product that depended on certain neuroses in society. At any moment, one or both of those factors could change.

The SIFT Coalition was thriving out of Sasha's three-story "Earthquake House." In the beginning, people flocked into the sprawling interconnected living rooms, drinking in Suki's art, listening to classical concerts, and joining in lively discussions about what problems needed solving and then, later, how to solve them. There had been a few tremors, but Sasha put off moving because he was so busy.

Keeping with the "Teal" organization idea, Sasha had created a structure for the SIFT Coalition that allowed new ideas to be born, built upon in tiered groups, and then distributed out to the world at large. He habitually consulted *Team of Teams*, by General Stanley McChrystal. The book challenged him to create teams that were nimble, transparent, and able to manifest solid decisions as cohesive groups. Sasha didn't believe in reinventing the wheel, but in refurbishing good tools to work with his goals and people. So, when he heard about a system or method for hiring and keeping good people, he tried it out. Eventually, using the Kolbe Profiles from Kathy Kolbe's book *Conative Connection* became second nature to Sasha and the WaterPurity Data managers. These profiles allowed him to assess each person's instinctive methods of operation and to pair them with team members who had complementary natural ways of doing things.

So far, Securing Individualism and Freedom Together had had the effect of creating awareness and conversation among American citizens about the scope and nature of their citizenship. At first, participants in the SIFT meetings weren't interested in using free enterprise to solve the nation's problems .

Sasha brought on a volunteer media person to put out print, online, and audio versions of news updates for each SIFT meeting. Things picked up when someone actually videotaped a brainstorming session on how to limit illegal immigration without involving the federal government. That YouTube video went viral, and the Associated Press picked up the story, reporting all over the world the aims and methods of the SIFT Coalition. Video presentation was definitely the way to go for maximum exposure. They now regularly videotaped brainstorming sessions and posted them on their website and on YouTube, inviting comments. Another person had volunteered to collect and catalog the comments.

As one company after another began to put the solutions coming out of the SIFT Coalition into place, the U.S. citizenry relaxed somewhat and turned a face of inquiry and acceptance toward the group. What was worse than not being listened to or accepted? The answer was, being so widely sought after that one got no respite. Sasha's phone and email had to be taken over by a team of 10 volunteers from local colleges.

Respite or balance from the ongoing demands was a high priority for Sasha. He went into meditation at 8 PM each evening and was asleep by 9:30 PM. He rose at 4 AM and was at his office by 9 AM each day. His offices had moved to the northern foothills, where it was quiet and less expensive to operate. Suki still lived nearby, but in her own home; she had actually purchased the family home she had been house-sitting in for so long. The family had decided to stay in Africa.

Obtaining office and laboratory space had taken a huge amount of money and time. Sasha knew that it had to be done, and he was glad to find an old air field with intact hangars that he could convert into manufacturing facilities.

He had relied heavily on Victor's guidance as he moved into deep financial waters. Without Victor's knowledge and steady hand, he could not have wrapped his head around the risk levels and how to leverage them best against profits.

The three years of his nascent business had passed for Sasha like a climb over a mountain when one is being chased by a mountain lion. If he had not had Victor and his mother and his friends to turn to for advice and nurturing, he could not have done it.

As he put out tentative queries about the possibility of setting up a micro-lending organization in the United States, he was instantly covered in regulations—literally, the printed regulations could cover his entire body. He discovered this one Sunday afternoon when he complained to Suki one time too many. She had quietly and carefully blanketed him in printed-paper regulations and then suggested they go for a walk. Suki and Julia still stuck by him, keeping his head on straight with their laughter and wit.

Sasha had never let anything drown his dreams, but the bulk of regulations associated with lending money had had such a dampening effect on him that he actually considered giving up. Sasha was determined not to be driven away by difficulties that were born from difficulties. If he did, he would be allowing the slow arm of corruption and government encroachment to choke the life out of him. He had several mantras that he used throughout the day: "The Lord is my shepherd," "I have no time or space to be offended," and "Om."

The four steps to success: Vision, Get comfortable being uncomfortable, Never give up, and Celebrate, were written in 10-foot letters on the outside of his company's buildings. Never give up. Never give up.

Just this morning, he had met with federal banking regulators to establish just exactly what he was going to be providing to borrowers. Thankfully, he was not in the business of making mortgage loans or even car loans. No, the loans coming from the Bank of SIFT were not going to be any larger than $1,000. They were designed to support small enterprises like taco trucks, daycares, jewelry repair and creation, pet services, maid services, landscaping, roofing, and so forth. Sasha already had a long list of companies and sole proprietors who had completed applications and were lined up to get going. The interest rate would be 3 percent, and the length of the longest loan was one year.

Of course, he needed the borrowers to meet in their groups regularly. He needed onsite observers to hold the borrowers accountable, and the borrowers had to use Profit Picture. Why not make such an insightful tool available to those who needed it the most? These small business people would be required to take the Profit Picture course throughout the life of their loan.

As for moral behavior, so far, the SIFT Coalition had influenced 4 out of 10 companies to change their bad behaviors voluntarily before the government made them do it. His days of disbelief about the crudeness and evil of mankind were long past him. Mankind was cruel and evil at times. It was a fact that had to be kept in mind. This was the impetus behind the Ten Commandments, *The Analects*, the *Bhagavad Gita*, the *Koran,* and the *Torah.* Evil lurked behind every choice, but so did Good. This conflict was the Play of Life, and he had gradually accepted life the way it was instead of holding onto an idealistic picture that disappointed him.

Another difficult realization was that common sense meant nothing to many, many decision-makers. He had reached the understanding that many people just wanted to fight against an authority. They didn't want harmony; they needed to fight the way Suki had needed to fight with her mom when she was 13. These people engaged through disagreement, never truly seeking a solution other than the chance to "prove" the opposite side wrong.

Gradually, Sasha experimented with reaching out to different sectors of society with the ideas germinated in the SIFT Coalition. Decision-makers whose businesses sustained low profits or no profits had no interest in anything except increasing their profits by any means necessary.

Those people making the huge profits were the most interested in independent action, especially if it meant avoiding bigger government intervention. Their companies had subscribed to SIFT Coalition blog. He was working on finding volunteers to produce an annual procedure manual that outlined all the details and steps involved in implementing the suggested solutions to business challenges.

For example, one SIFT idea was how to keep Child Protective Services from breaking up families. The SIFT Coalition suggested that Nonviolent Communication, Nonviolent Problem Solving, and Nonviolent Parenting be three courses offered in every middle school and high school during the summer and required for graduation.

The students' families would receive a 10 percent discount on their car insurance for each class completed in a given year—or discounts on mass transportation if they didn't own a car. The classes would include, as the participants aged, discussions about communication and problem solving in family, work, and social situations. Several municipalities had implemented this idea and had asked for support in creating the curriculum. Sasha put out a call for volunteer curriculum writers, offering work experience and barter for other services, but no pay. He was intent on keeping the SIFT Coalition completely free from the exchange of money.

Finally, after moving from one demographic and industry and self-defined group to another, he had cobbled together the types of people and types of gatherings that one could really call "seeds."

These were sometimes young people, sometimes deep thinkers. The majority were second-generation immigrants whose parents had escaped extreme threat or hardship. This group included all ages and both genders. They grew up hearing their parents marvel at their good fortune to be in the United States. Like Sasha, they grew up sensing a veiled threat behind their parents' eyes. Among the young, he'd discovered a new voice in America, a voice unafraid and eager to believe in freedom from tyranny. This was the voice of true patriots, people who embrace and strive to maintain the spirit of the Founding Fathers: Risk everything, expect no handouts, fail or succeed on your own results.

The angry fighters with political pedigrees and suitcases full of jargon and speeches left as soon as they realized that they would have to contribute ideas that worked and that they would not be given a platform in the meetings or form a new political party through the SIFT Coalition.

As he slowed down to drive through the flat, treeless streets of Borrego Springs, he wondered how the water table was doing. He'd heard that the golf course had drained the town's water for its grass.

Sasha parked his car and walked through the cacti to Nur's door. It was open, and he could see her in the kitchen making tea. He stood watching her for a few minutes, thinking he was unseen. Her head was slightly bowed over the cups, and she spoke with her back to him, "You left your lights on."

Turning back toward the car, he sighed: Still the spy.

He returned and joined her, as he had imagined he would, on the patio to watch the sun dive behind the massive cliffs and boulders.

She turned on the LED candles and brought out spicy black bean sauce over rice and crispy walnuts.

They ate, only speaking to trade jokes. That was the standard dinner with his mother, only jokes and lighthearted laughter. He liked it, and she seemed pleased never to speak of serious matters again.

Or so he thought.

She poured a small glass of plum wine for him, taking only lemon tea for herself.

"Let's go inside," said as she stood up, wrapping herself in a white wool shawl Victor had given her.

Sasha tilted his head questioningly. His mother often sat outside all night. She hated to leave the stars, especially when he was visiting.

They went into the living room, which was as round and as small as a cave. It would have been a cave except for the skylight and windows. Nur put a log made of coffee grounds into the fireplace and lit a fire.

He sat down next to her on the floor, and they watched the flames.

"I have never told you the story of my . . . my wedding to Victor."

He perked up. "No. No you haven't. Are you going to tell me now?"

She nodded and flashed him a big smile. "Yes."

"Shouldn't Victor be here?"

"He knows it."

Sasha shrugged, "OK, Mother."

She began slowly, tracing a circle in the white carpet with her finger. "You remember the picture of Victor standing by the circus zoo in Russia?"

He nodded. "Yes."

"That was taken in 1994. He finally managed to leave Switzerland with the gold and return it to the right people. It wasn't easy. The way he got out was the way he got in, by Saint Bernard dogs hauling it on a sled. The gold was in bricks. He walked down to a goat trail and made a deal with the herder to bring him five of these animals and a sled. It was the same way he got there, and the herder was the same man who took him in. They had a deal that, surprisingly, worked out."

She continued, "When he got to the town, he slept in a barn with the gold. It was wrapped in bags to look like seeds. He told everyone that they were poppy seeds going to Afghanistan for the heroin trade and that was why he had to hide." She shook her head again, saying, "They believed him. After all, he was Russian, and he looked like a typical runner. He spoke Pashto and Dari, had a long beard, and wore a scarf on his head in a manner that would probably convince a Swiss goat herder. Of course, he also paid him."

Sasha nodded, of course.

"Anyway," Nur sighed, "he made his contact after a month of sleeping in the barn and a truck came down from Zurich to pick up the gold. He got his share and a passport back to Russia. I met him there, in Moscow, and we talked for a long time. He had had a religious experience, a spiritual experience," Nur said and looked at her son.

He nodded, "Yes, I know, Mother."

"We . . . finally decided to marry, even though we knew that we would be separated. We went to the circus, you saw that. What you don't know is that the zoo is, was new. They tore down a twelfth-century cathedral to build it. Underneath the zoo are what we would call catacombs. There are some burial areas, other areas for meetings, and areas for storing artifacts. Most things have been looted, but there are still beautiful drawings and writings on the walls.

"We met a young man who took us into the tunnels through a hidden door inside the bear's cage, below the bear's sleeping area. We walked for at least a mile through the tunnels. I don't know if we could have found our way out. Finally, the guide brought us into a wide open space, and there were about 30 people—mostly Russians but some Afghani and some Indian people. They were Christians, and most of them had come through a different tunnel they had dug over the course of many years. I didn't ask and they didn't tell." She paused and Sasha could see that she was determined to tell him the whole story.

"They were burning candles, and I saw...." She stopped again and gazed into the fire.

Sasha knew that his mother sometimes had spiritual visions. Most yogis did if they practiced for a long time because their intuition became sensitive, and they often realized things beyond the capacity of logic.

"What did you see?"

"I saw," she said as her voice broke, "I saw Babama just standing there looking at me. He was glowing a little bit and . . ."

"And?"

"And, I saw your master, Jesus Christ. He held out both of his arms to us, welcoming us." She turned to Sasha, smiling. "It was such a relief for me," she said. I had a small doubt if it was right to marry Victor, but when I saw them, I knew it was OK—even if we had to be apart, it would be OK. So . . . we came and stood among them. An old woman, a Russian woman, put a beautiful piece of lace over my head, and she gave me a braided red thread and she gave one to Victor."

"A braided red thread?"

"It is called a kalava in India. It signifies union and respect for God. When the woman ties it around the man's wrist, she is asking for his protection. When the man ties it around the woman's wrist, he is asking for her loyalty. These strangers had come all this way and even brought something according to Vedic belief for me." Nur's eyes grew shiny with tears. "It was the most wonderful experience of my life," she continued, "to be there among them, the candles, the sight of my beloved father, and the Christ. To marry after so many years of waiting for Victor; it was so wonderful for me Sasha." She shook her head and smiled. "Little did I know what would soon follow: years of raising our child with another man, and having to escape to safety in the United States. I often wished I had never left those tunnels . . . but then, I submitted to the spiritual lessons of this life at a young age." She smiled as if laughing at herself a little bit. "An ancient saying is, 'We are all women with God.' That means we are all receptive and following. We do not make the plan, we follow the plan. Today is modern. You would say, 'We are all female energy with God.'"

"Mother, what about all those years with me and Yusup? What was that like for you?"

"It was . . . it was a spiritual task. I had moments of enjoying life and having fun, but for the most part, I worked to be kind and to show Yusup a way of being that was loving and caring. I had to teach you many things so that you would grow up to be a man of wisdom."

At these words, Sasha put his hand over hers. "Thank you. You did show me."

They sat looking at the fire for a long time. "Mother, why are you feeling today that you must talk? I am so glad to hear, but I wonder what makes you tell me now?"

"When we had been married for five days, I received a summons to return to China. When I got there, I was told to marry a Uyghur man. I think that they knew I was involved with Victor and they sent me on the assignment to keep me away from him. I don't know for sure, because there was unrest and the government was behind the genocide. They incited the Han Chinese, even paid them to hunt down the Uyghur people. By having me marry a Uyghur man, I would probably be killed. I would have, you and Yusup would have died, but there was an American who helped us."

"Who?"

"He was a man I met briefly in Germany at the same time I met Victor. His name was Richard. Richard was a banker running an American bank in Beirut. I met him by accident one day on the street. I tripped in the street and he helped me up. That is all. Then he bought me a coffee and showed me pictures of his wife. When I realized that he ran an American bank in Beirut, I knew that he was acting as an informant for the CIA, that he was also a spy. I desperately wanted to defect—the Chinese were threatening me at every turn, but I couldn't defect in a café. I gave him my name and phone number and asked him to give me his. He did, and we parted ways.

"When the killing started, I contacted Richard and Victor. They worked together to get us all out. Richard was our friend. He even helped Victor come to the United States. All this time, Richard has protected me from being discovered by the Chinese government. He masked my identity."

"What happened to Richard? Did he die?"

She nodded.

Sasha's face grew stern and he asked, "What does that mean, Mother? What happened to Richard?"

"Even though he was not a government employee, he was still a spy. When he retired to a ranch in Texas, he got a mysterious illness and soon died. He told me when he moved that he knew the U.S. government would not let him live."

"Really?"

"Yes. It is an old story. The governments destroy those who know their secrets."

"Mother . . . ." Sasha didn't know what to say. His throat contracted painfully.

"Remember to guard against strong attachment," she warned him. "Everything that happens is the right thing, even if we do not think so. It is. This life is not your personal wealth. It belongs to God, and you spend it as He decides. You do not deserve anything. Everything is a gift, especially the chance to serve."

He nodded. He went into the quiet place, the hiding place within his heart and determined to hold fast to that peace no matter what. "Mother, remember the game you taught me? Remember the presents you wrapped up and gave to me?"

Her face in the firelight became animated and she laughed. "Yes. Sasha. I was such a serious mother. Please forgive me. I . . . I knew that I was living in such peace and freedom on borrowed time. I wanted to tell you everything before I had to leave."

"Mother, are you going to . . . will they kill you now that Richard has left his body?"

She nodded and put her tiny hand to his cheek: "The time has come."

He began to sob, and she stood up quickly, "Come on. Let's sit outside now and watch the stars all night together. You cry when I am gone. Now, just be happy together."

He walked with her back to the patio looking out over the desert and sat down. She sat next to him and folded her legs up in the lotus position. She wrapped the white shawl around her and straightened her spine. Within minutes, she was deep in meditation, her breath nearly stopped, her consciousness soaring toward God.

He texted Victor: "Come to Nur's house now."

Sasha laid his phone on an opaque glass table and also straightened his spine. He breathed deeply and gradually became calm. He closed his eyes and lifted his gaze to the point between his eyebrows, the spiritual eye. It was midnight then. At three o'clock in the morning he opened his eyes and looked at Nur, she was motionless and white in the night. Even though the air was quite cool, sweat ran down her face—a face that radiated joy. He stared at her beautiful plain face for a long time and realized the truth of what she had said. Everything that happens is the right thing because everything leads us to God.

He turned his gaze to the stars for a long time, getting lost in the sky. It seemed like 10 minutes had passed when Sasha looked away from the stars and back to his mother. Her upper body had slumped forward. She was dead. He could see the tiny dart in her neck . He searched the dark desert with his eyes but could see nothing. There had been no sound, not even the breaking of a twig or the wind.

He carried her inside and laid her on the bed. Immediately, he noticed that her room was full of packed and labeled cardboard boxes. He found a key next to a metal box in which were bundles of thousand-dollar bills.

Sasha locked all the doors and called Victor again. "Hello? Is she gone?" Victor's voice was calm and quiet.

"Yes."

"I'm coming around the mountain."

"Victor, should I call the police?"

"Yes. Hang up and call them now."

Sasha spent the next hour with the sheriff and his deputy. They took the dart, and the coroner's office sent a car for the body just as the sun came over the mountains. Victor's car pulled in next to the coroner's. He spoke with them and then came inside. They embraced. For two days they grieved together in her house, talking things over.

"She used to keep boxes wrapped in gold paper and ribbons in the closet, like . . . wrapped gifts."

"What for?"

"When I was a kid, if someone did something to me, like, hit me or cut me down or something like that, she would hand me a box and say, 'It is a gift to be hurt by someone else because then you can forgive them.'"

"What did you do?"

Sasha laughed ruefully, "I threw those gift boxes in the trash! I could not follow her logic. Usually, my mom made sense to me, but this present stuff did not make sense."

"What do you think of it now?"

"Now?" He hung his head between his shoulder blades like an old bear and sighed. "Now, after the goddamned Chinese have murdered my mother?" He wiped the tears from his eyes and looked up at Victor grimacing in pain, "Now . . . I . . . understand." Victor put his arm around him, and they sat before the fire that they fed continuously.

"There's half a million dollars in there."

"Yep. She left a will. It's a college fund for the kids in her Kyrgyzstan village. She wants you and me to administer it."

At the end of the second day, the San Diego County coroner's office called to say that Nur had a highly toxic poison pooled in her neck but that she had actually died about five minutes before the dart hit her: the cause of death was a heart attack, or cessation of heart. Sasha realized that he had turned to look at her just as her soul was leaving her body. What joy she must have felt at that moment!

Victor thrust his fist into the air and said, "Yes! They didn't kill her. She left her body in peace. She wasn't murdered! Yes!" His eyes were alive with a grieving man's last triumph. He and Sasha laughed deliriously for a few moments. Nur beat the Red Chinese!

Then Sasha became solemn and grabbed Victor's arm. "Tell me. Tell me the truth: Are you next? Richard, Mother, and then you—is that how it's going to be? Please tell me! I have to know."

"No." Victor ripped open a bag of marshmallows and began sticking them onto coat hangers he'd straighten into skewers . "No way. I'm a . . . how can I say this? I'm a failed spy, Sasha. Your father never made it to the dangerous secrets. After I lived with gold in a mountain, during which time the Soviet Union changed political systems, I emerged to be a sort of administrative errand boy. No, I do not warrant murder. Certainly, if they were going to knock me off, they would have done it after I came back to work in 1994." He shrugged. "There are worse things than being a bad spy." He winked.

The made s'mores and slept on the floor in front of the fire.

"Hey," Sasha turned to him before dropping off to sleep, "remember when you were Crandall and I sat in front of the fire in London?"

"Yes. I remember."

The next day, they put the fire out and packed the boxes in their cars. They picked up Nur's ashes at the funeral parlor and took them out to the top of the highest cliff they could see from her house, where they tossed them out in handfuls, yelling Nur! Nur! And they watched the ashes float down, down toward the ocean of sand. Sasha had found two braided red strings in an envelope with his name on it, and he tied one on Victor's wrist while Victor tied one onto his.

"With these strings we remember the Divine presence and we remember Nur and we promise to keep that remembrance all our days."

That was two days ago.

Home again in the pink and yellow rooms of the Earthquake House, after a long day at work, Sasha let his mind retrace the events of his mother's life. Tomorrow, he would make plans to travel to her village with Victor. Tomorrow, he would file the SEC and Federal Reserve papers to establish the SIFT Micro Bank to be based first in the highly depressed cities of Carthage, Mississippi, and then in Baton Rouge, Louisiana.

Tomorrow. He pulled out the crumpled, stained pages of his original business plan as he lay on his bed. It seemed so . . . over-the-top now. He hadn't written a second book. In fact, he hadn't written any poetry in three years. There were many things he thought he would do that reality had not permitted. Still, by writing down his aspirations, he had been able to realize many of his dreams. Sasha knew that he would complete what he had written in his plan, including the micro-lending bank and the water data test, and more that he had not yet conceived. He was most passionate about the SIFT Coalition. Everything in his life came down to two distinct missions: spiritual communion and rigorous exercise of civic duty.

"Every second, a new citizen is born; every day, an existing citizen finds their voice." He sat up in bed, groped for a pen, and wrote that down. "Note to self, tweet this. Possible permanent tagline for my life."

References

Adler, Mortimer J. 1972. *How to Read a Book: The Classic Guide to Intelligent Reading*. New York, NY: Touchstone.

Blanton, Don. MoneyTrax, Inc., training materials.

Cheney, Lynne. 2015. *James Madison: A Life Reconsidered*. New York, NY: Penguin Books.

Coolidge, C.J. 2008. *The Squaredime Letters*. Friendship, TX: Long's Peak Press.

Daniels, Mitch. 2011. *Keeping the Republic: Saving America by Trusting American Voters*. New York, NY: Penguin Group.

Ho Xuan Huong. 2000. *Spring Essence*. Translated by John Balaban. Port Townsend, WA: Copper Canyon Press.

Kolbe, Kathy. 1997. *Conative Connection*. Phoenix, AZ: Kolbe Corp.

Lawrence, Brother. 2009. *Practicing the Presence of God*. Rockville, MD: Wildside Press LLC.

McChrystal, Stanley. 2015. *Team of Teams*. New York, NY: Penguin Publishing Group.

Sullivan, Dan. Strategic Coach®. www.strategiccoach.com. Accessed Sept. 19, 2016.

Wagner, Hazel. 2009. *Power Brainstorming*. Barrington, IL: B9D, Inc.

About the Authors

Michelle Boyd Photography

About Ron Schutz

After being trained in problem-solving techniques as an engineer and receiving a commission in the U.S. Navy Reserves, Ron pursued his passion for banking and finance by completing his Master of Business Administration at New York University. Now, after being immersed for a half-century in the financial world, he relives his challenges through Sasha's struggles and Victor's life experiences.

Ron consults with business owners and their key profit makers to help them realize their full financial potential. He has a natural tendency to develop strategies and see workable solutions in preparing companies for transition.

He lives in Houston, Texas, with his wife, Gail. Together, they have four children and three grandchildren. Working in small groups within their church community occupies much of their free time. Ron is also a trained Stephen minister, a lay caring ministry that provides one-on-one support for people working through a crisis. www.stephenministry.org.

About Laura Baker

Laura Baker lives in Lockhart, Texas, where she runs Vida Equilibre Activities for Girls (vidaequilibre.org), an after-school program for the daughters of incarcerated women. She wears many different hats while bringing this program into operation: ghostwriter, teacher, and videographer for The Messages Project, a sister nonprofit that is also focused on serving prisoners and their families.

Morgan James Speakers Group

www.TheMorganJamesSpeakersGroup.com

We connect Morgan James published authors with live and online events and audiences whom will benefit from their expertise.

Printed in the USA
CPSIA information can be obtained
at www.ICGtesting.com
JSHW022342140824
68134JS00019B/1634